Hearts
And
Flowers
Coloring
Book

By Artist
Dwyanna Stoltzfus

Join the Fun!!
Share your colored pages!!

You are invited to color the pages
From this and all publications by
Dwyanna Stoltzfus. Then scan and post
Your colored creations in
"Coloring with Dwyanna"
Adult Coloring Group
On facebook
https://www.facebook.com/groups/1519357628356169/
Join Coloring with Dwyanna Adult Coloring Group,
And have fun sharing your colored pages
And meeting new coloring friends.
Members of the group will also have access
To free coloring pages.
You are welcome to share your colored pages on
Any social network, make sure to mention the title of
The book and the author/artist name.
Uncolored images may not be shared.

Acknowledgments

Thank You to my family for all your support of my
Art and this project. I could not have done it without you!!

Thank You God for the gift and love
Of art and drawing!!

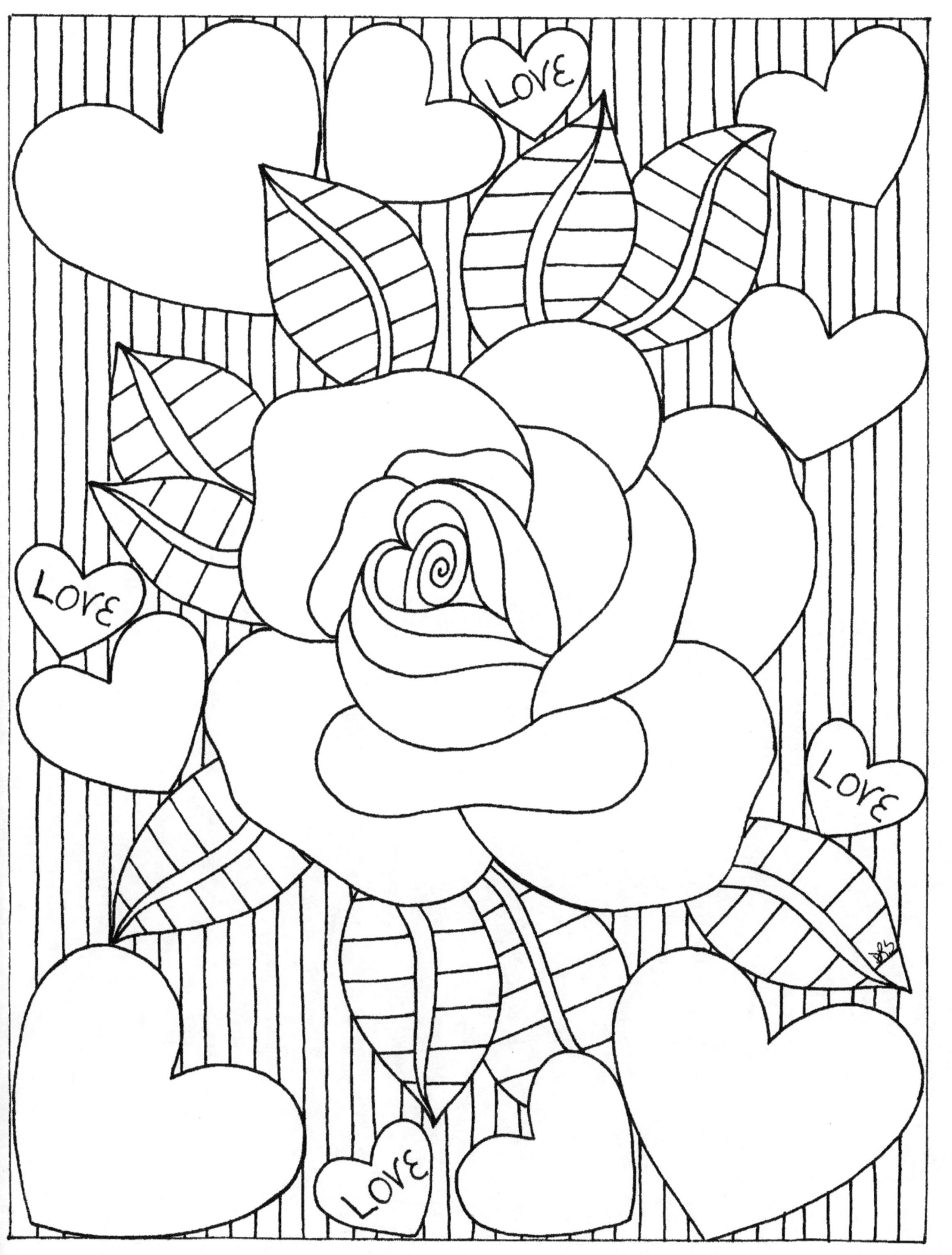

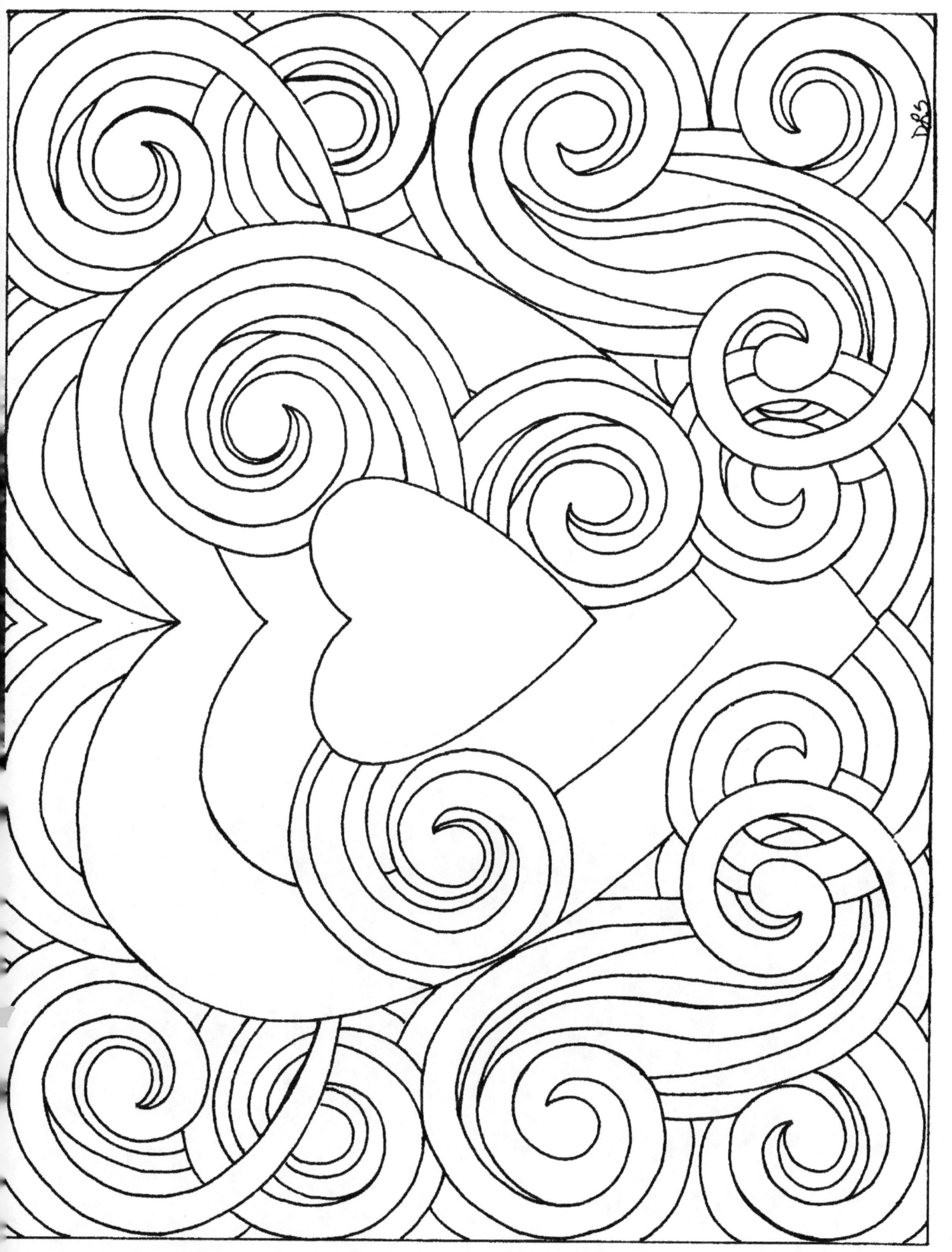

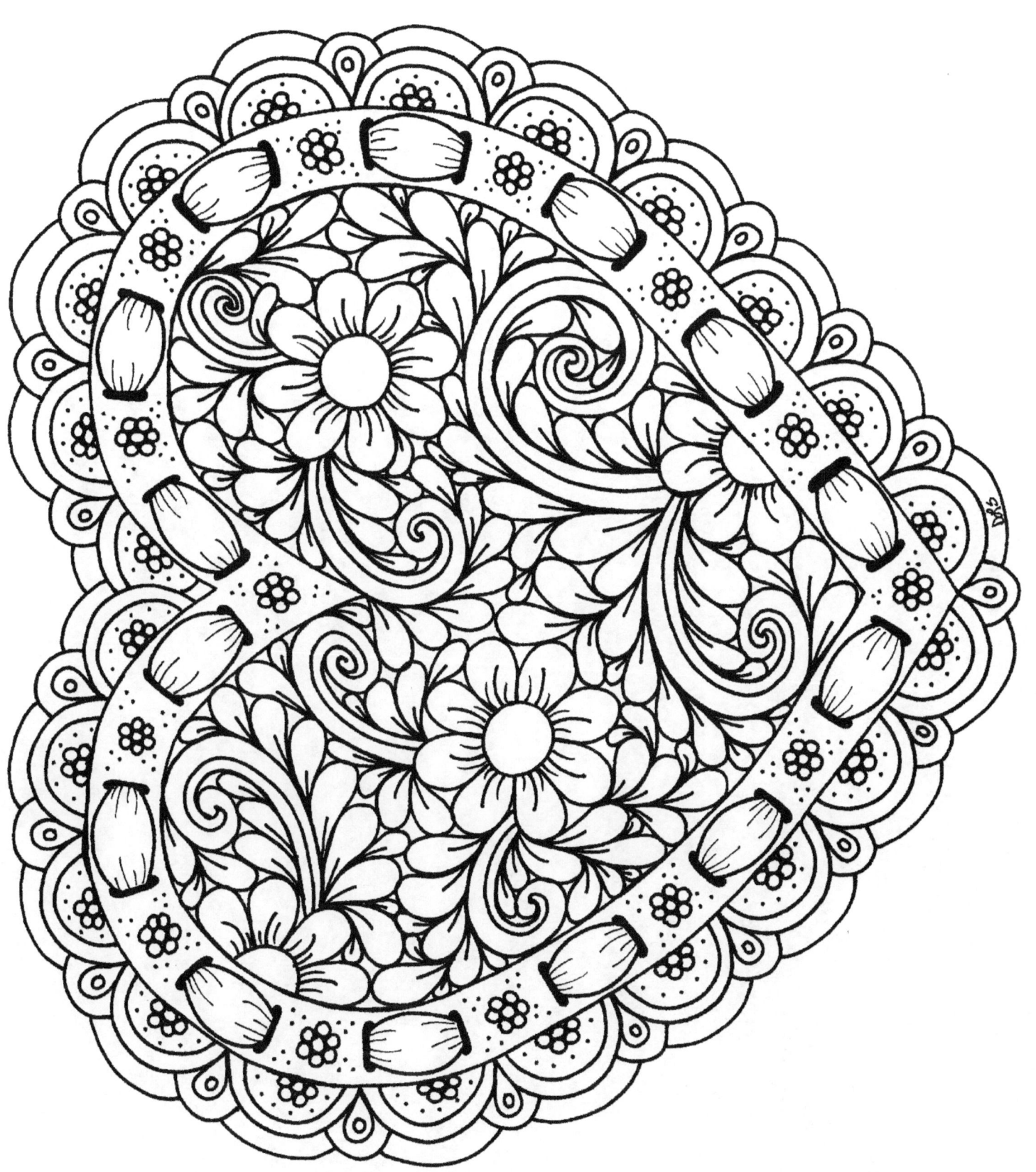

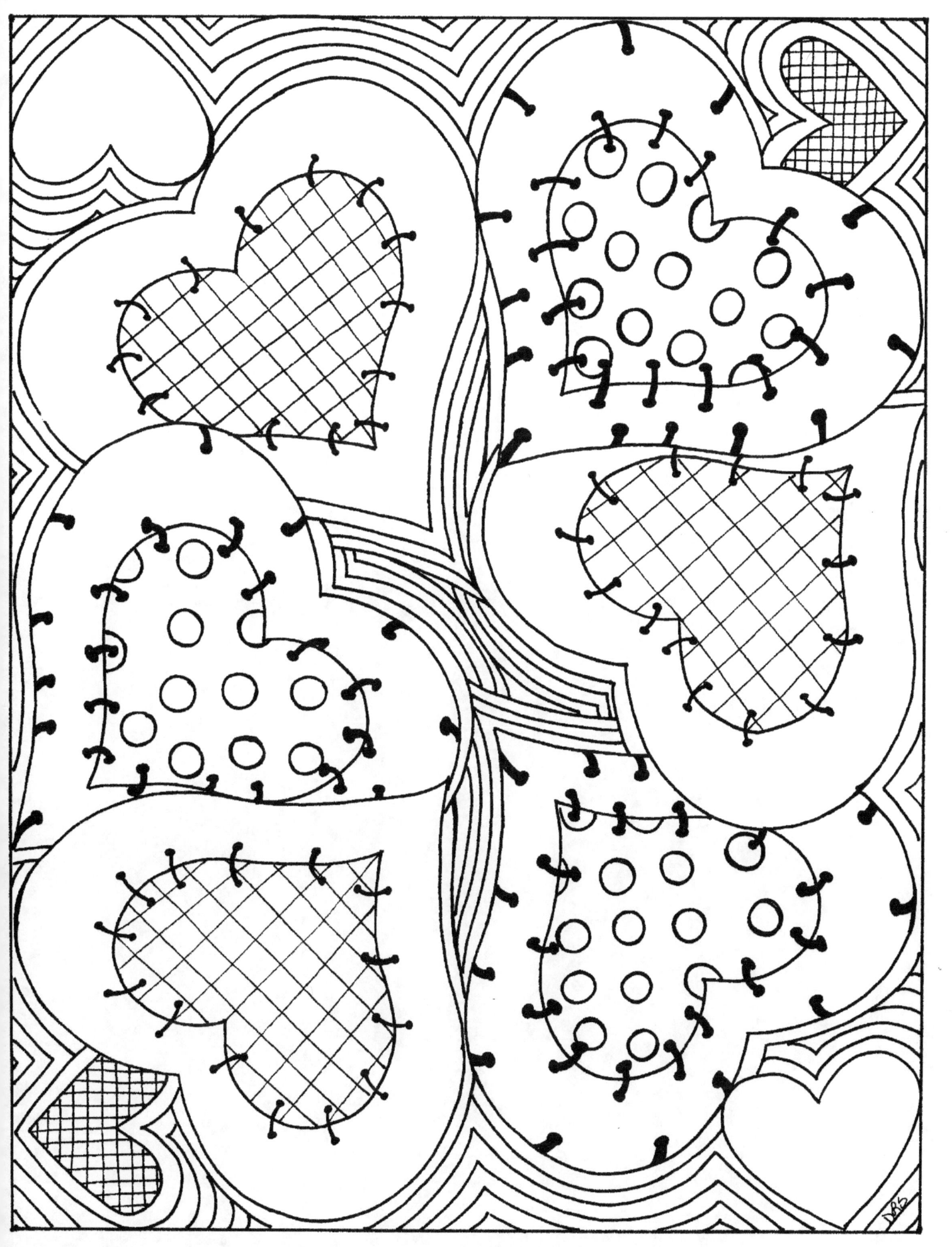

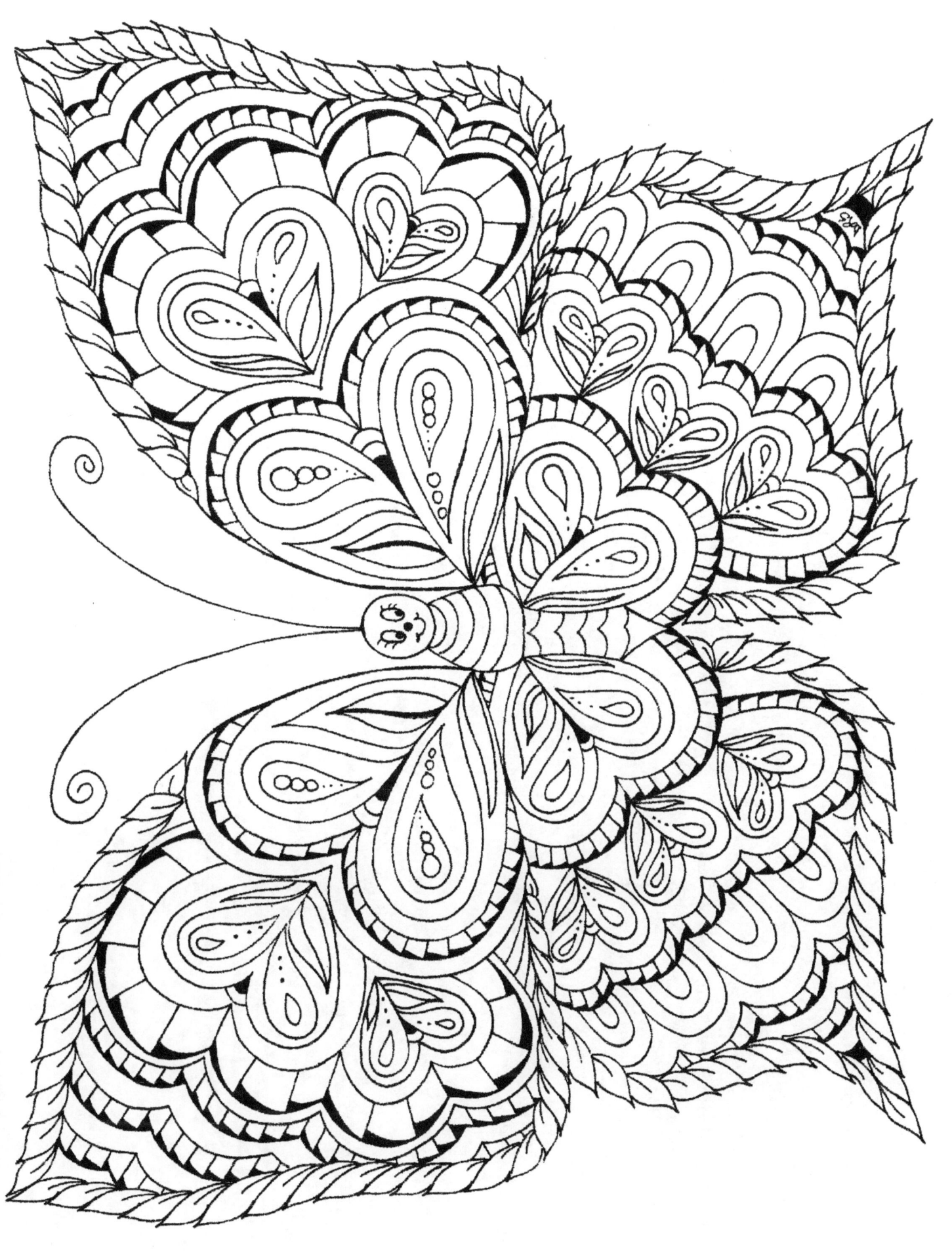

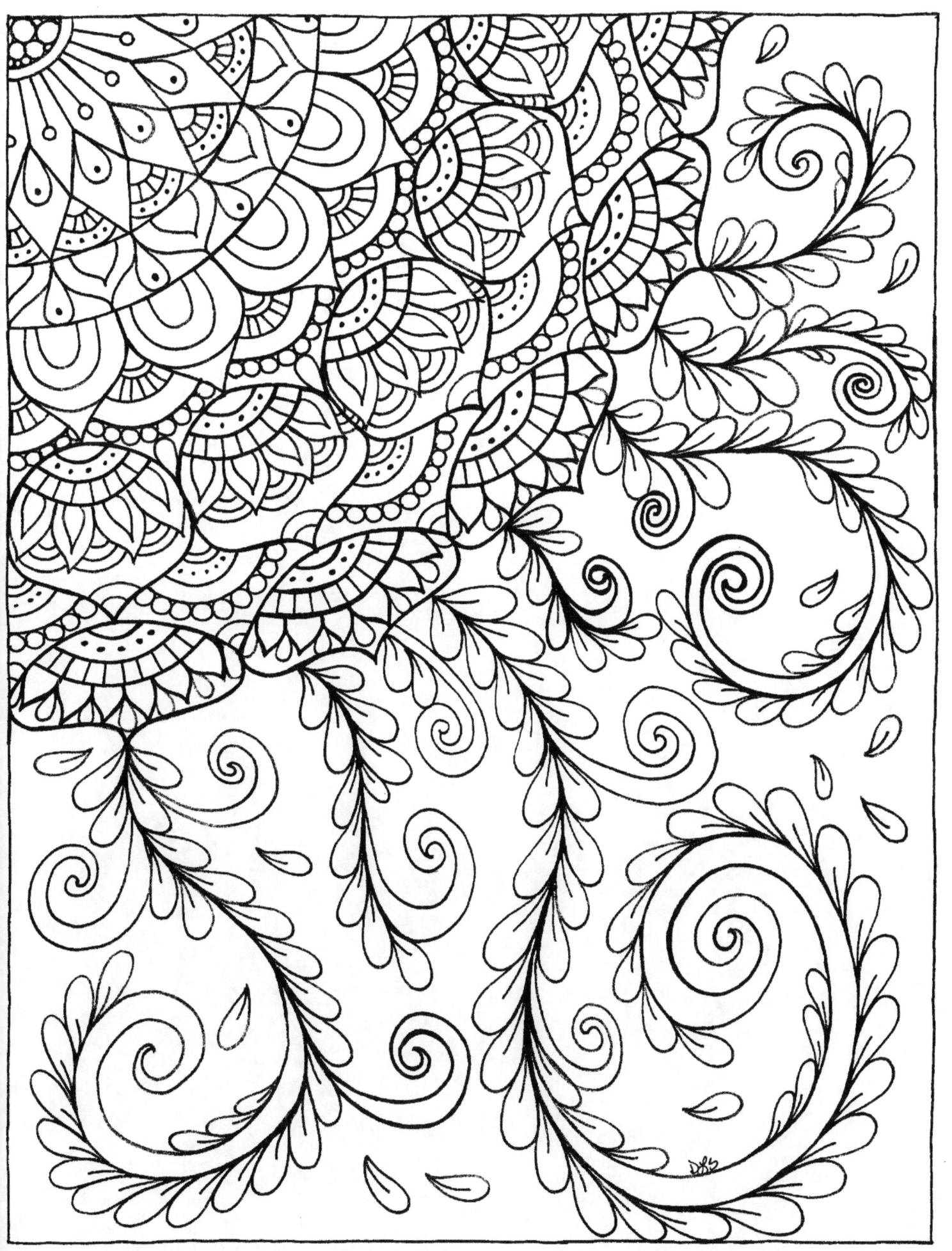

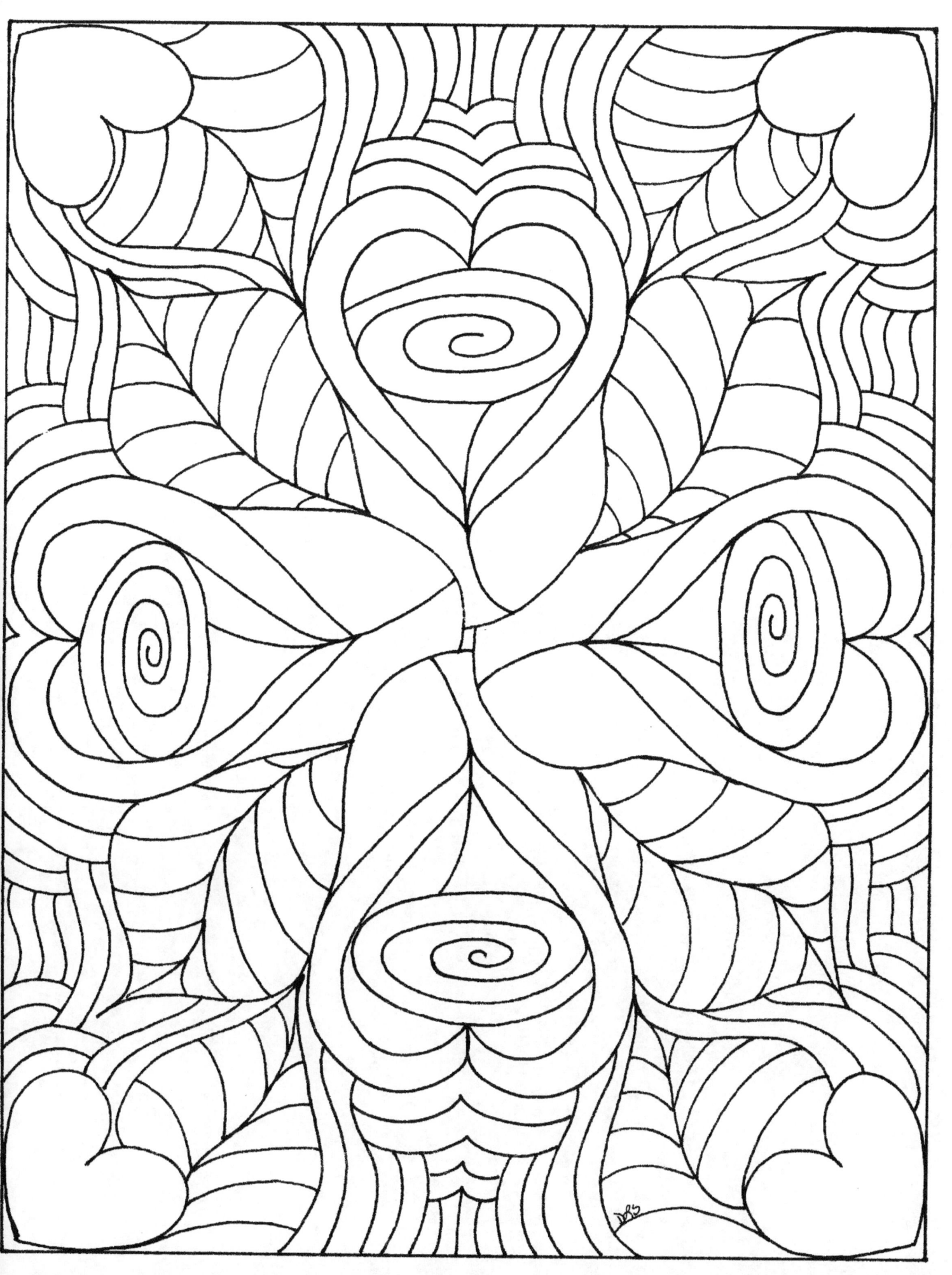

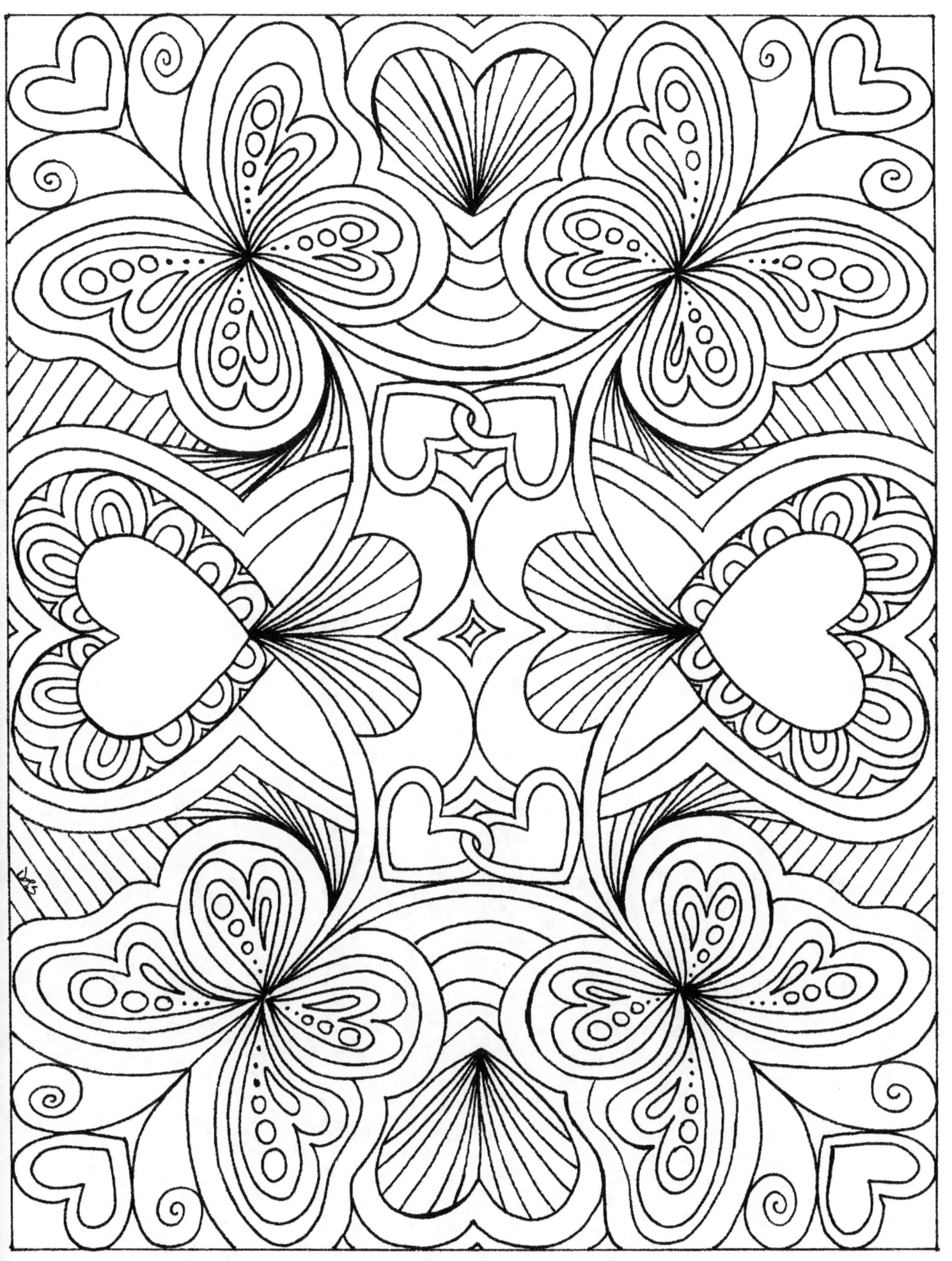

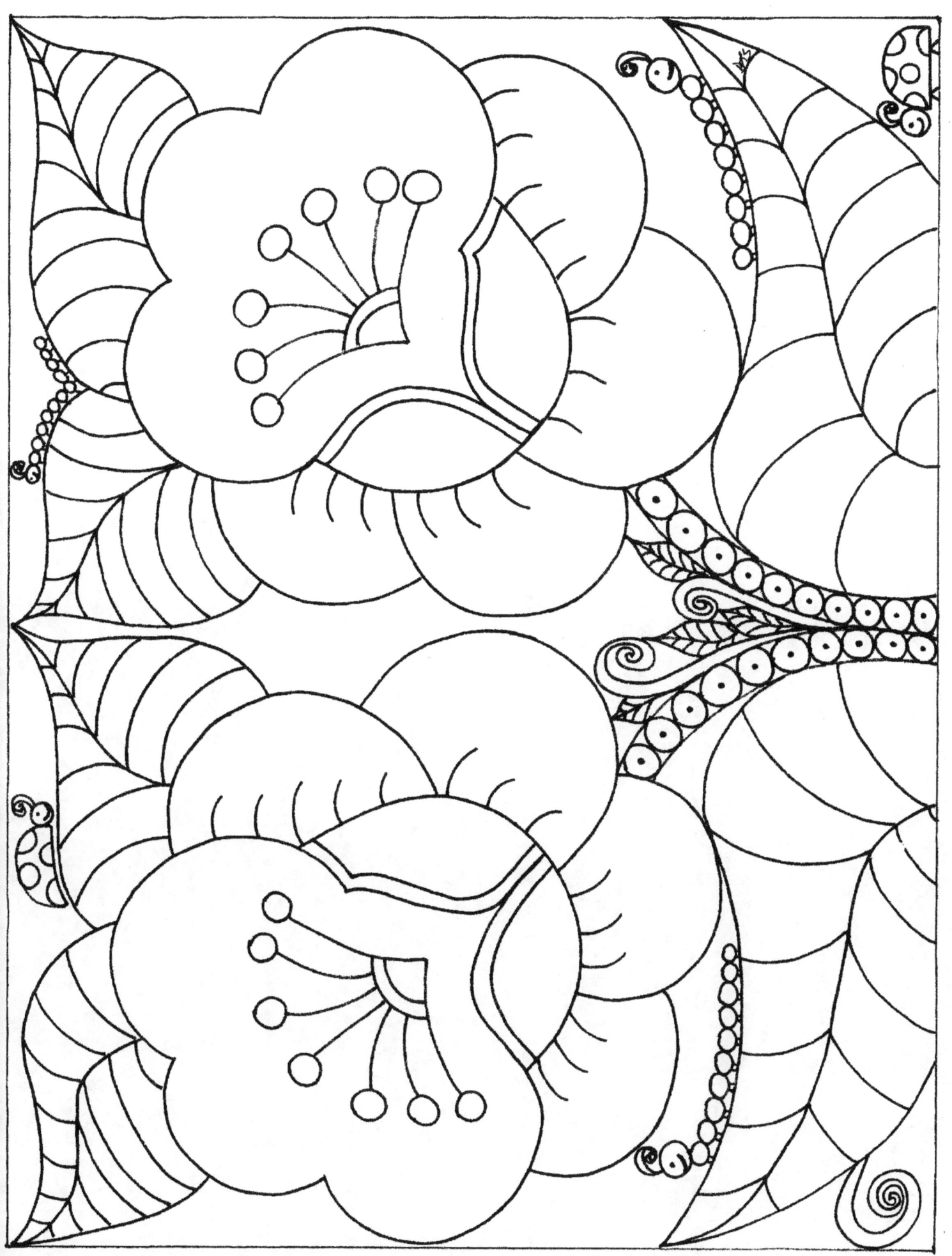

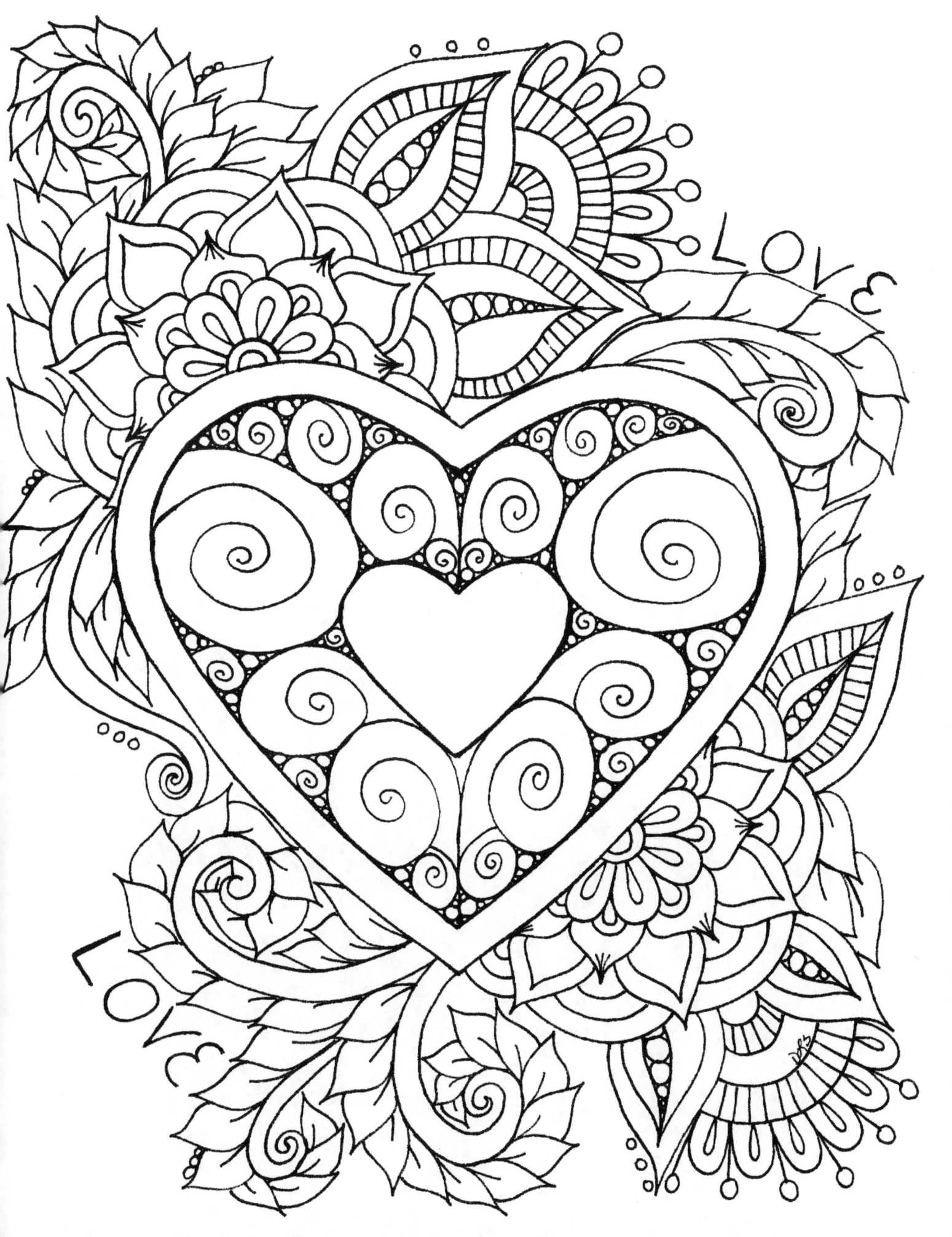

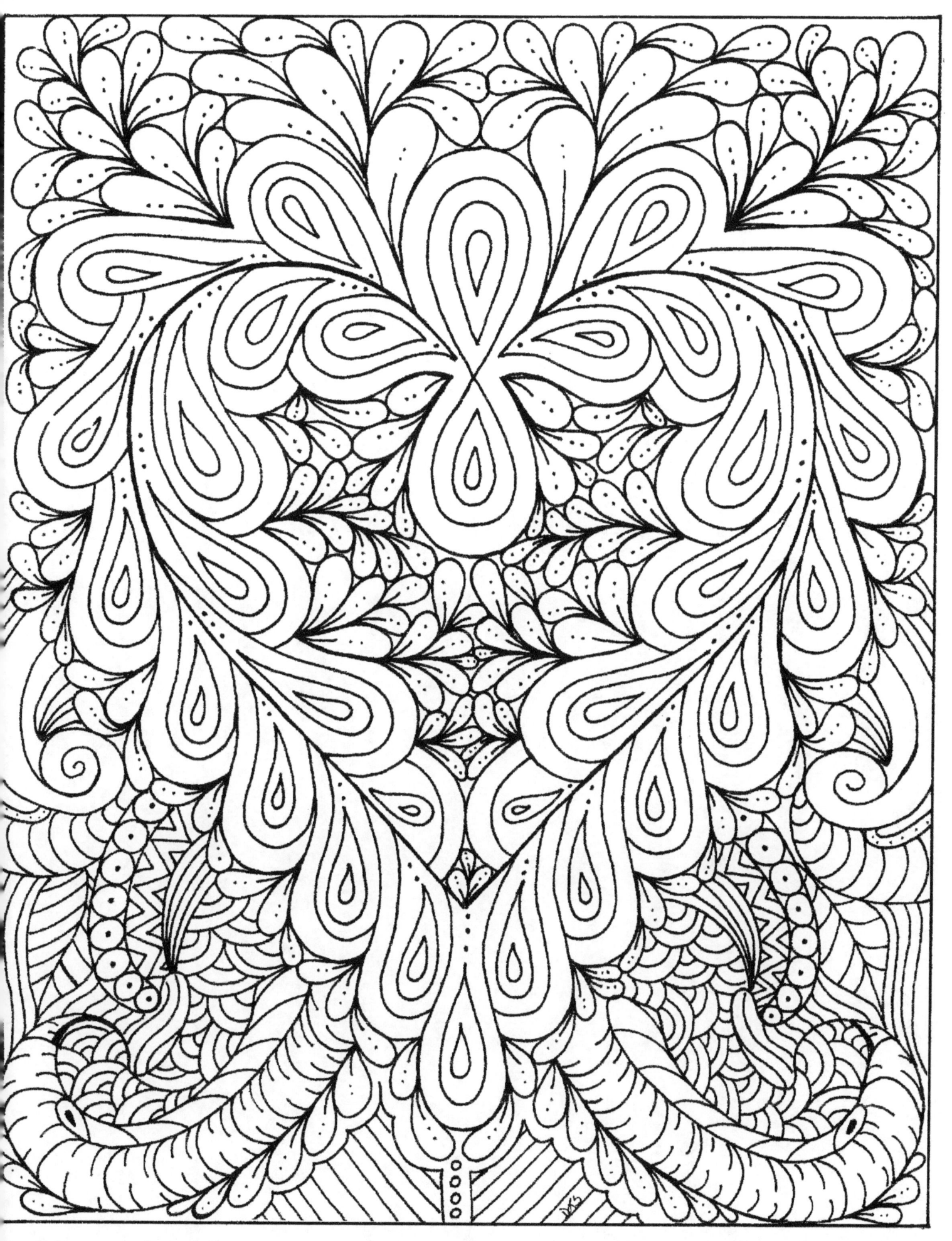

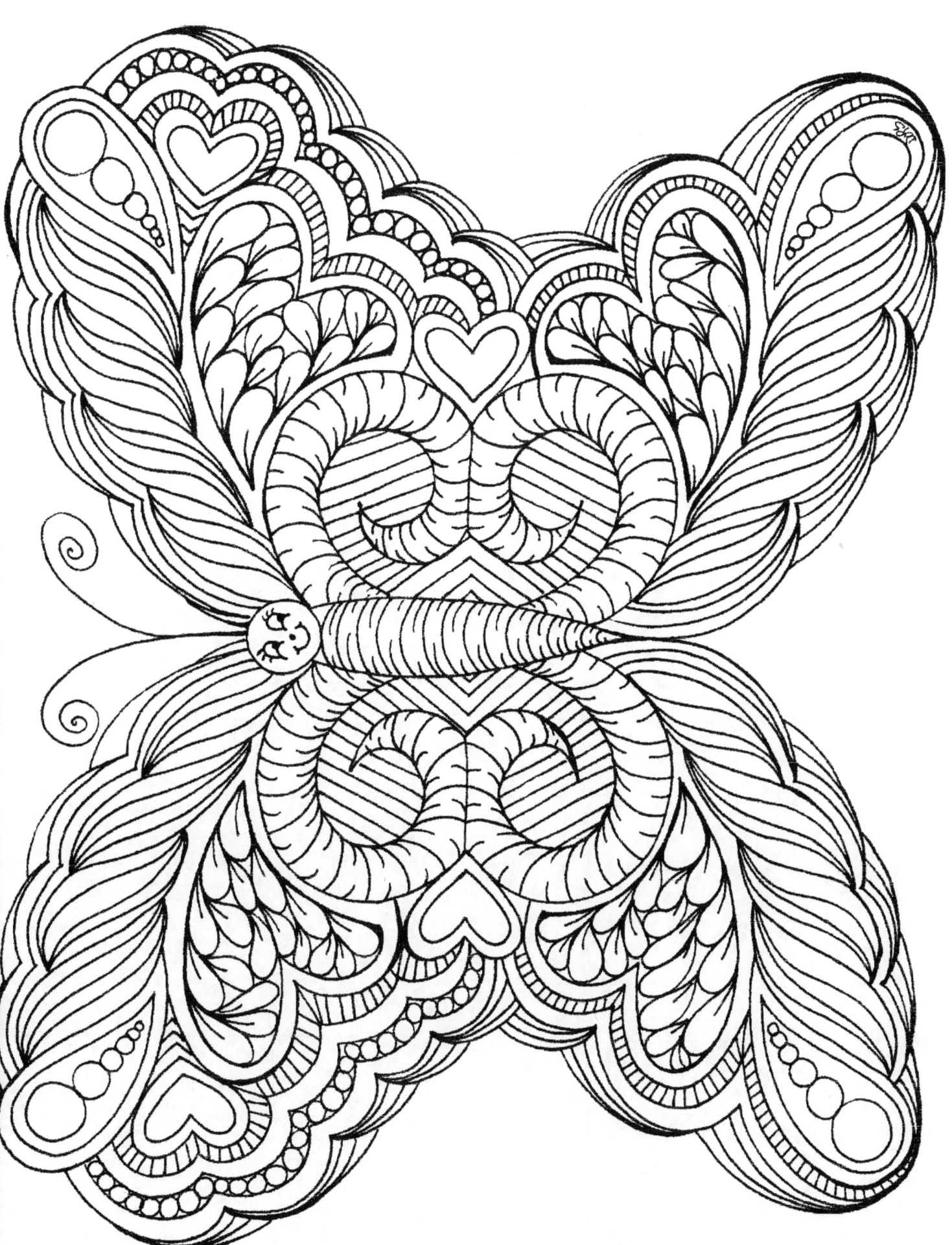

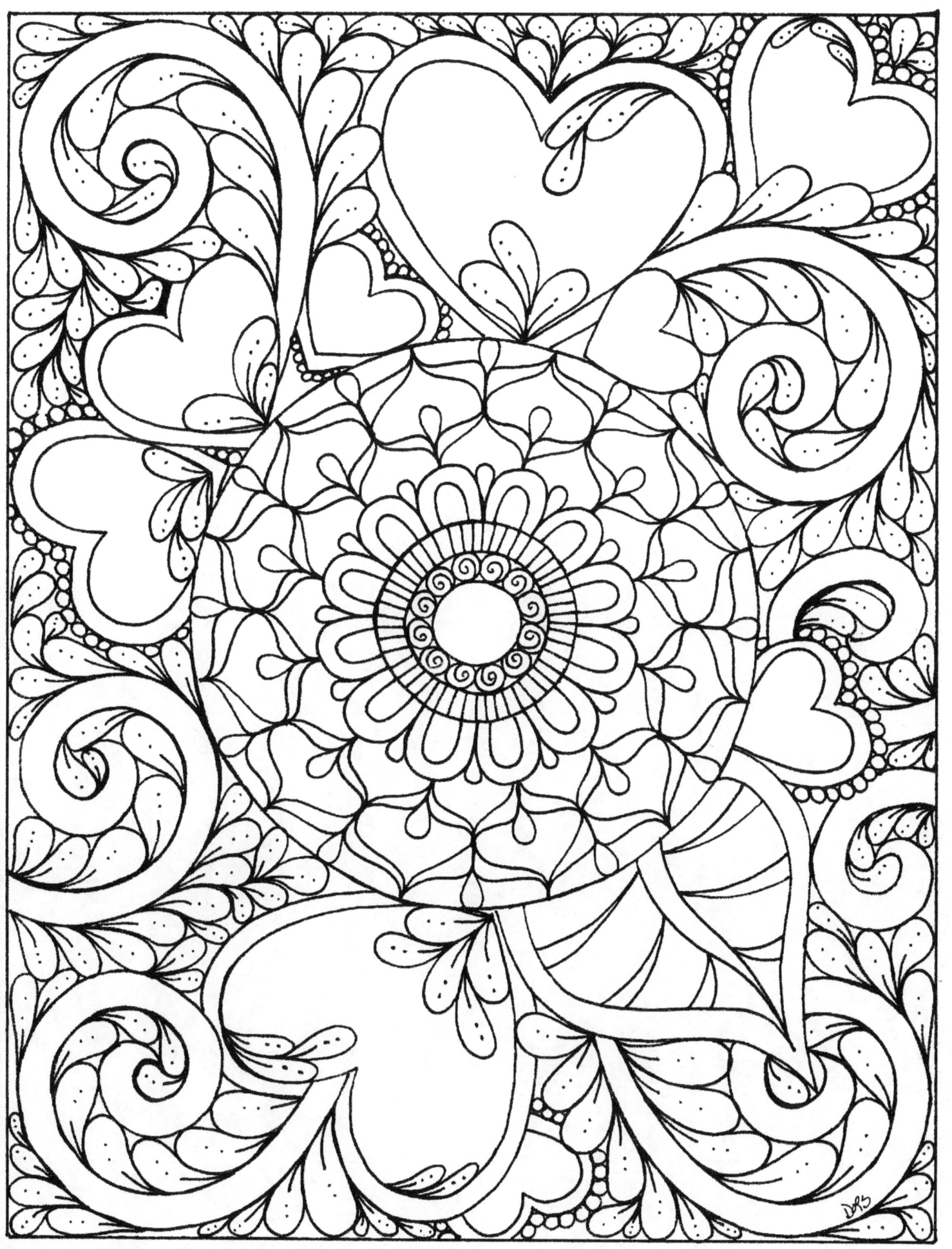

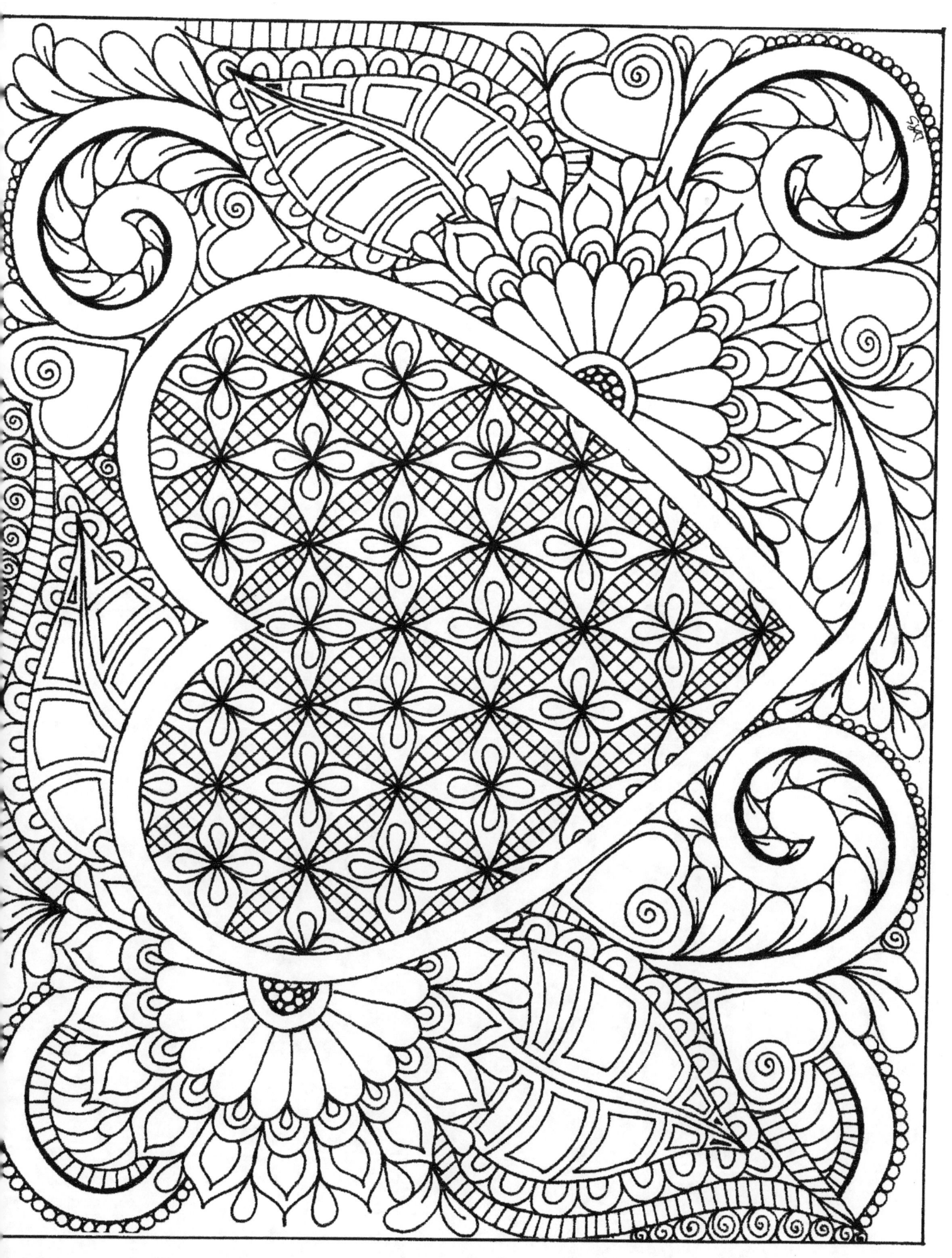

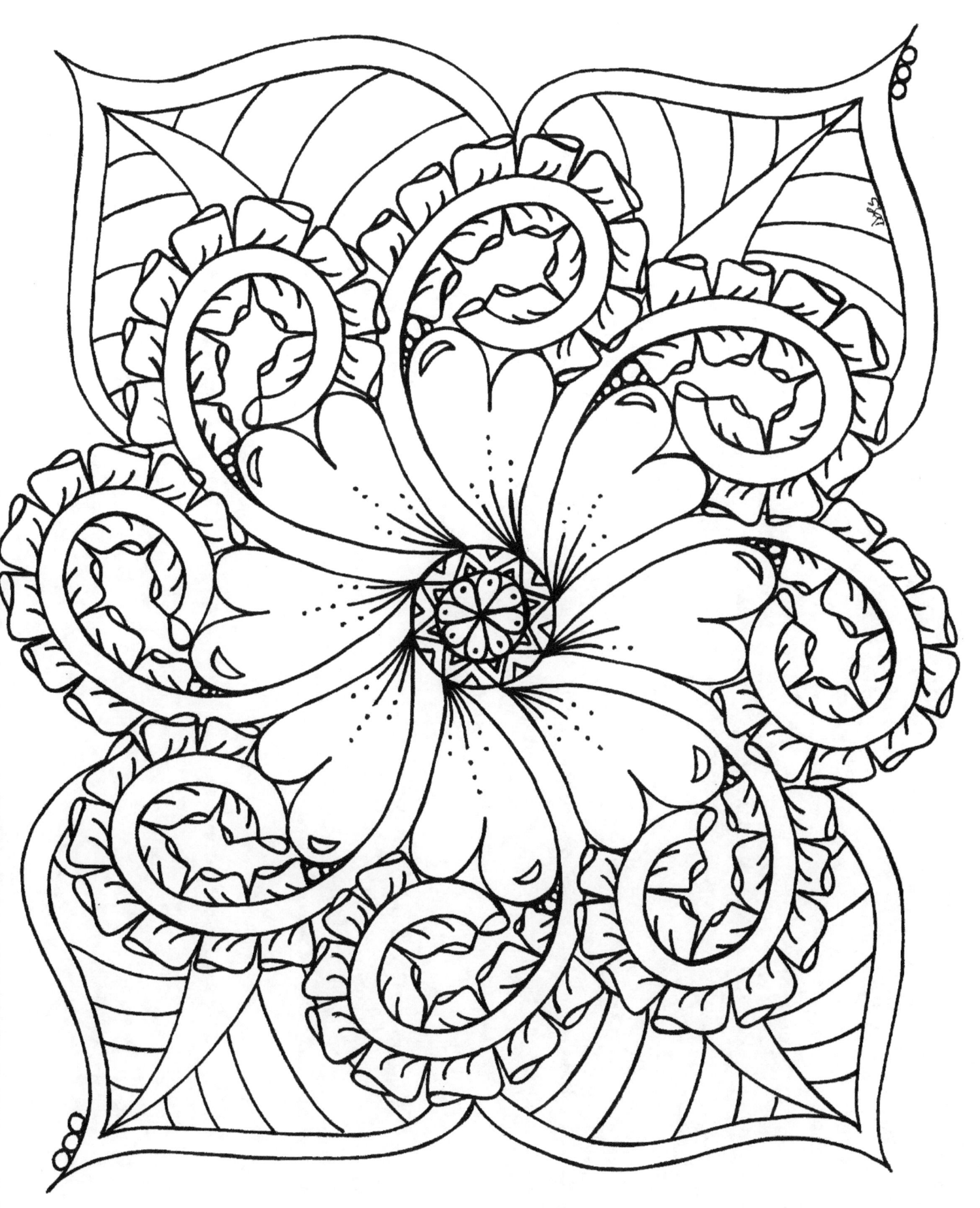

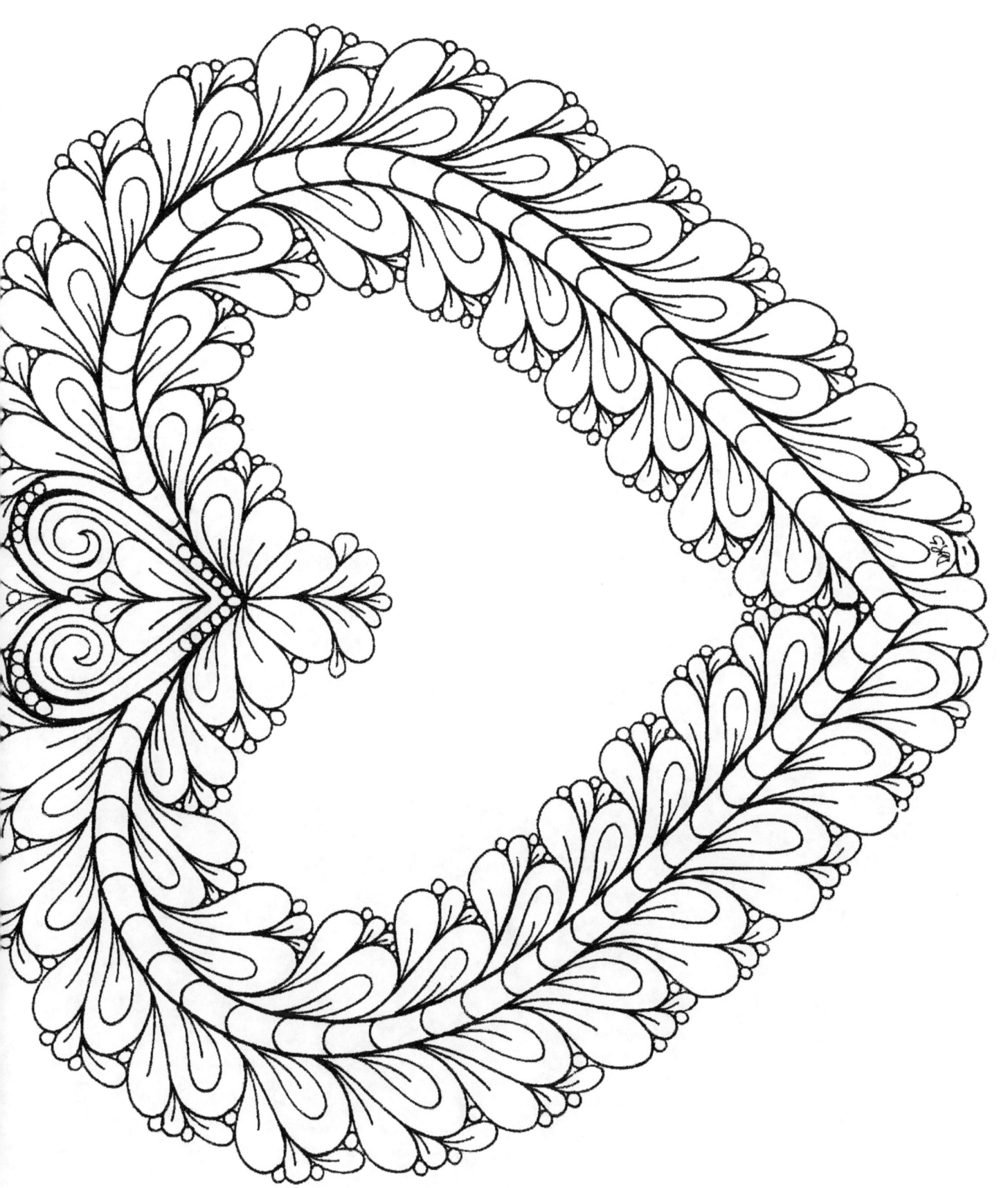

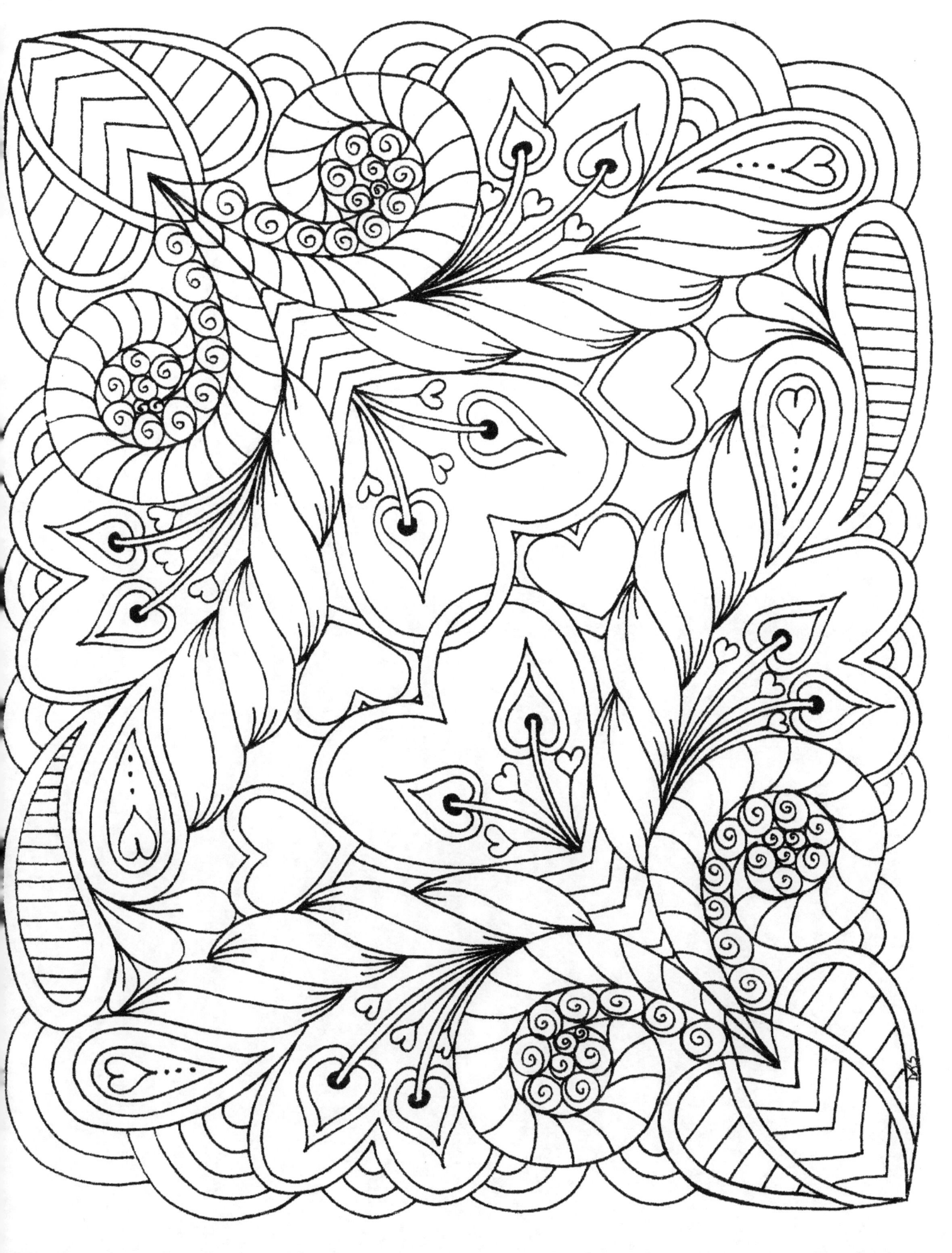

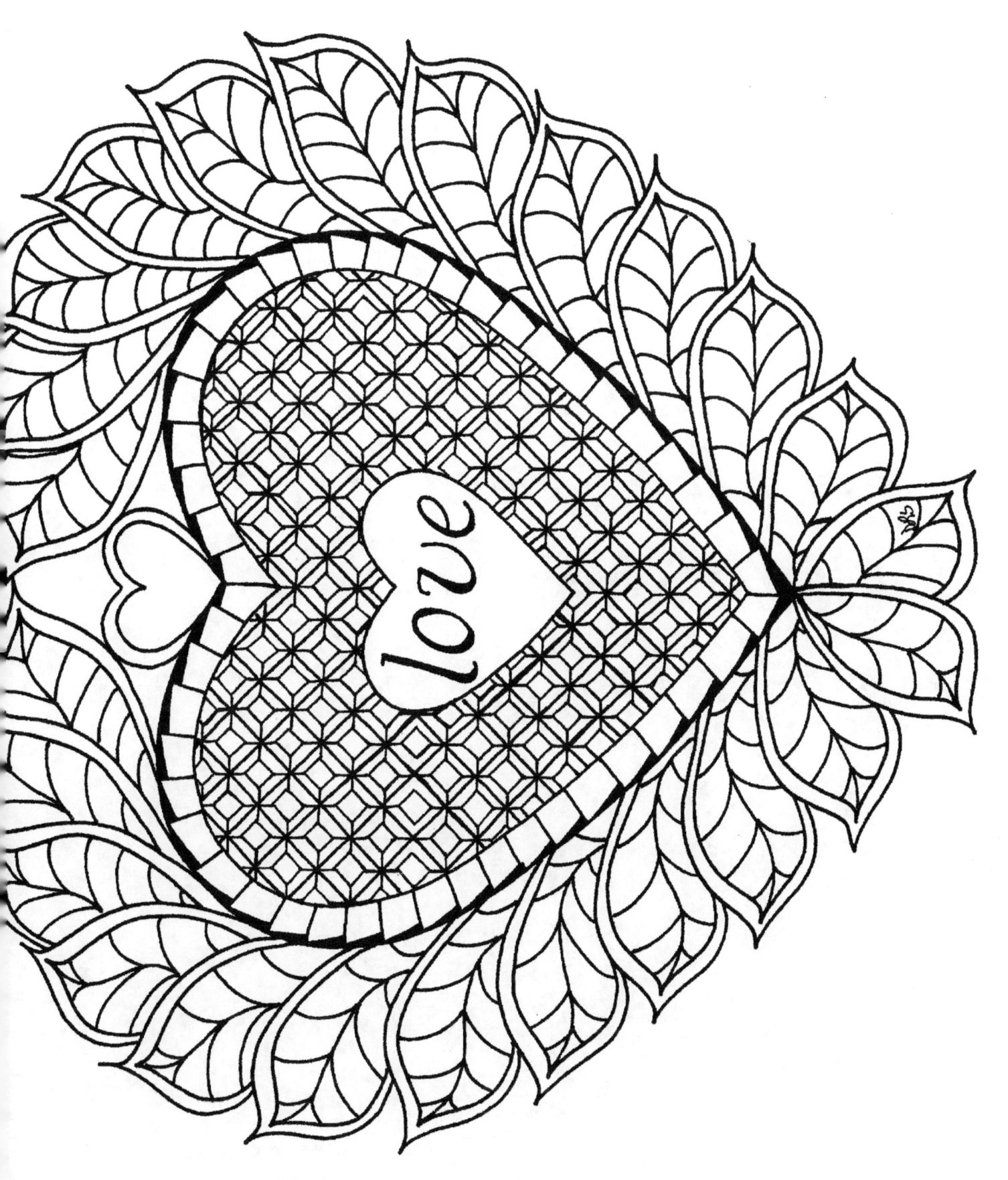

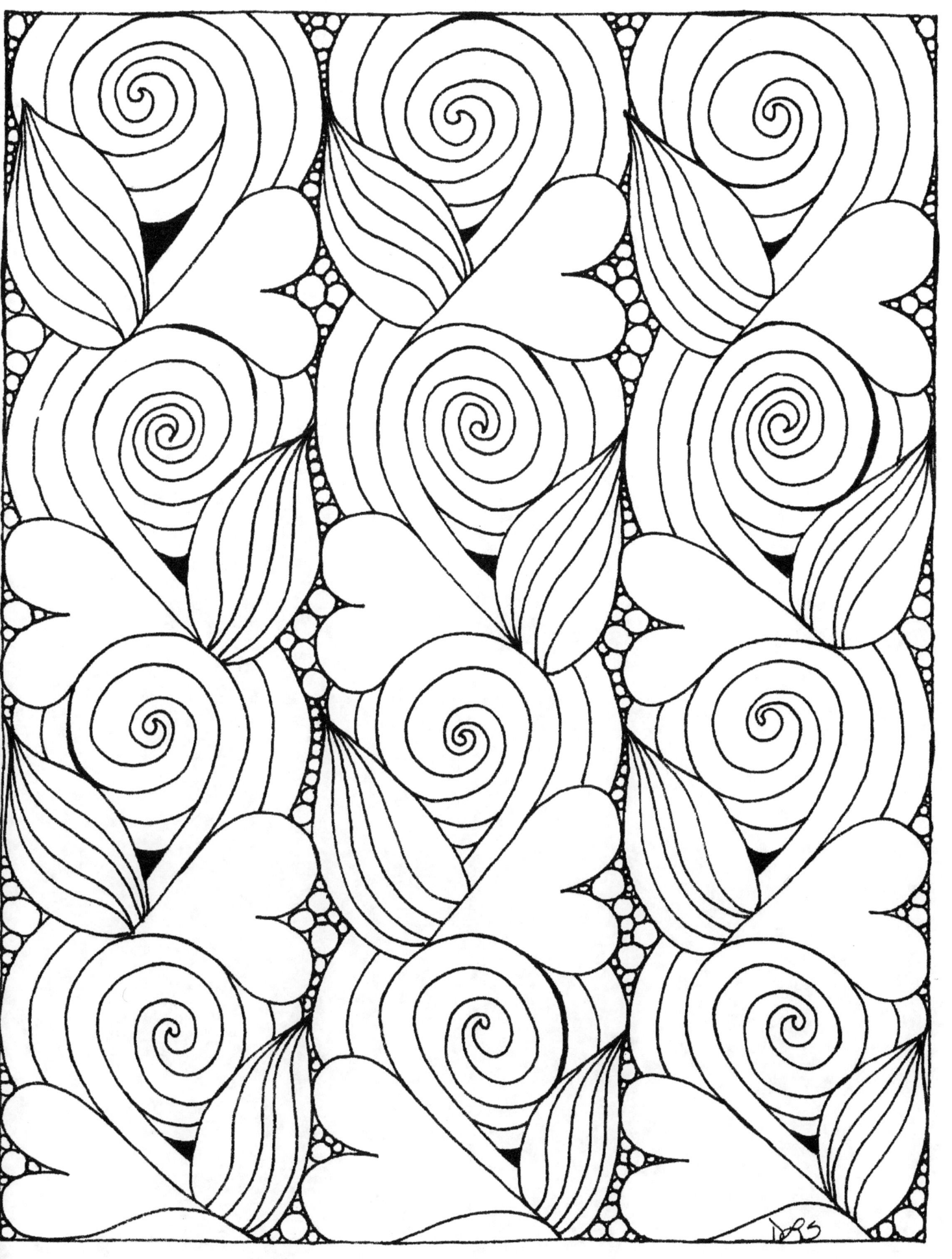

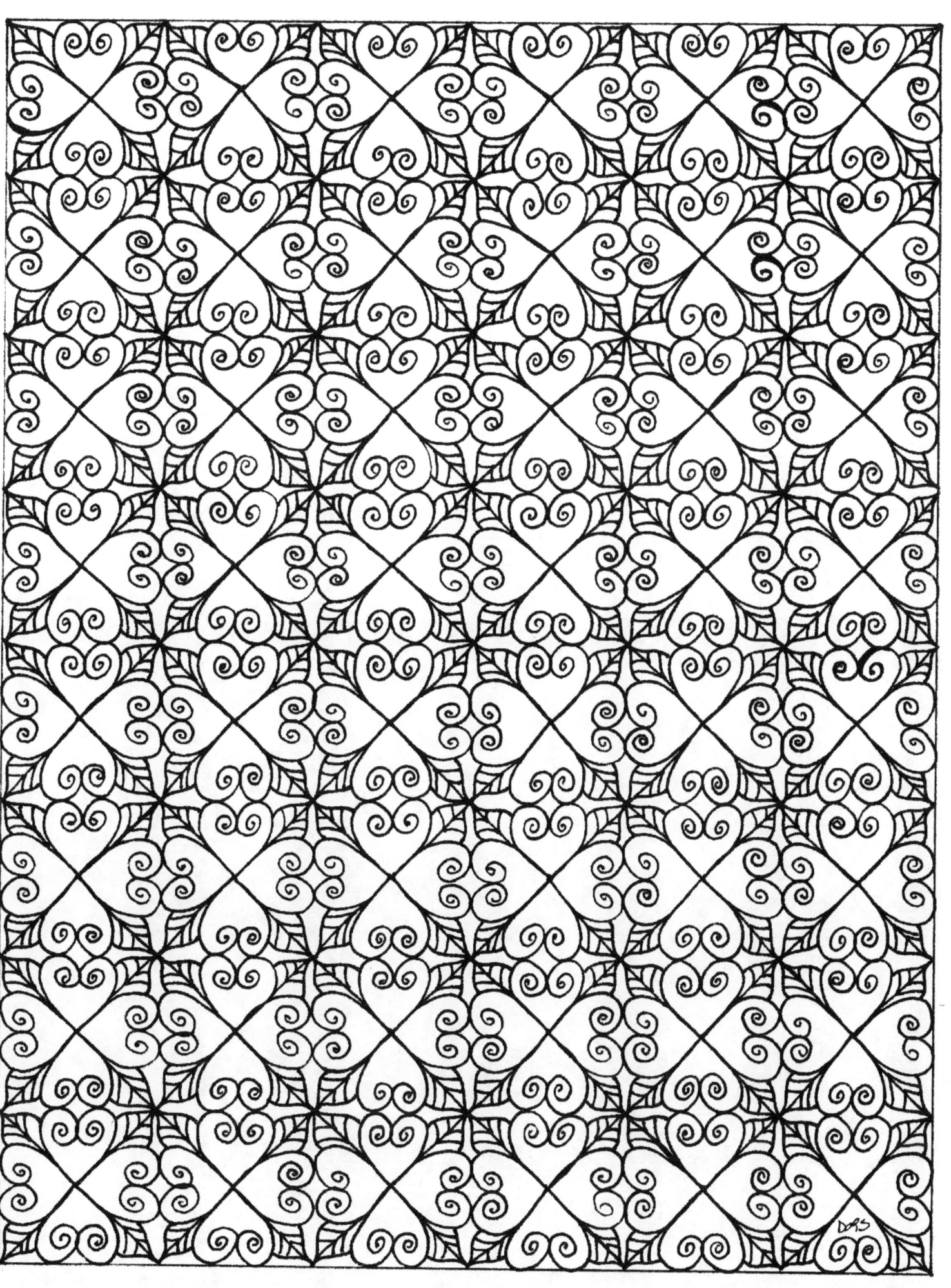

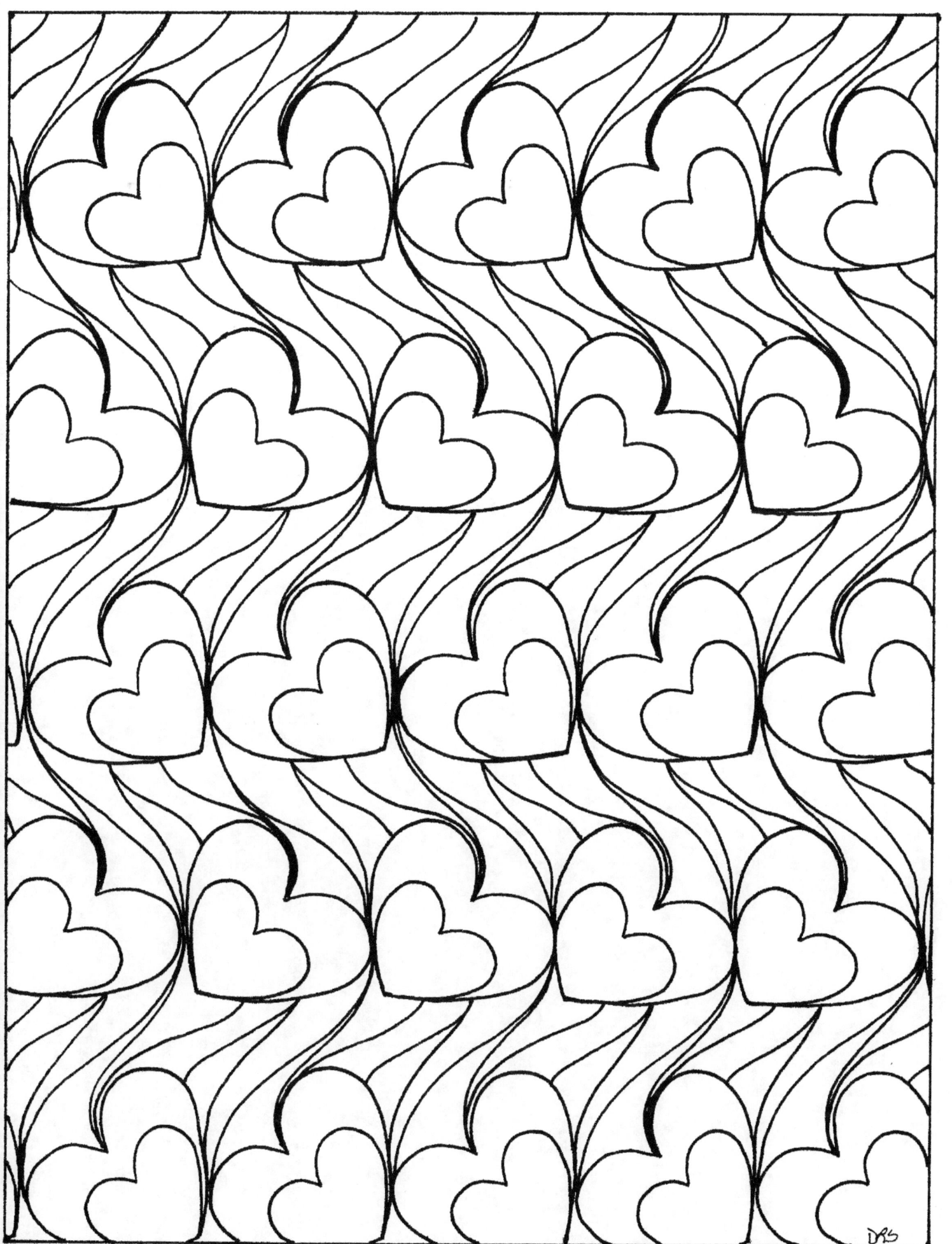

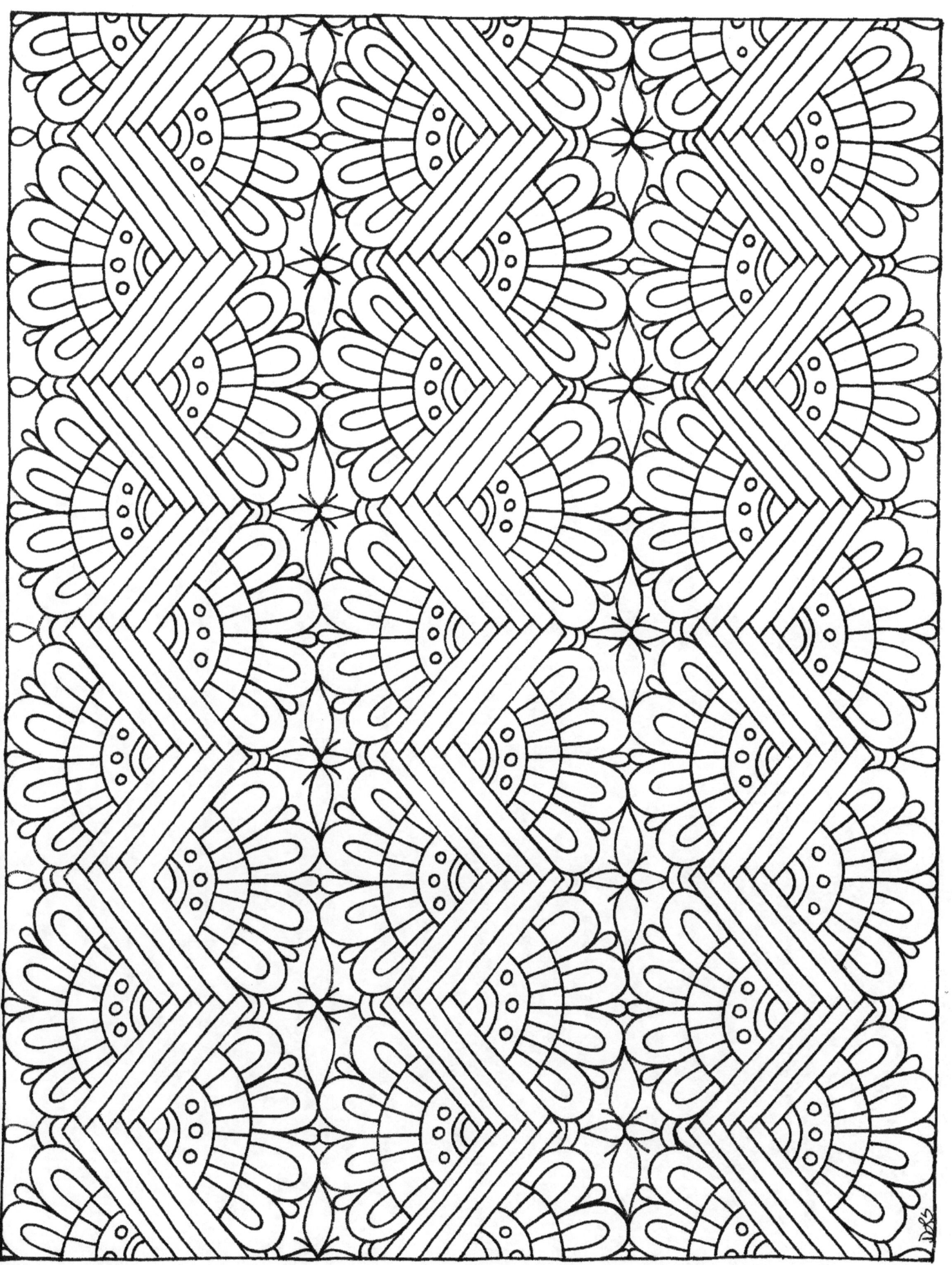

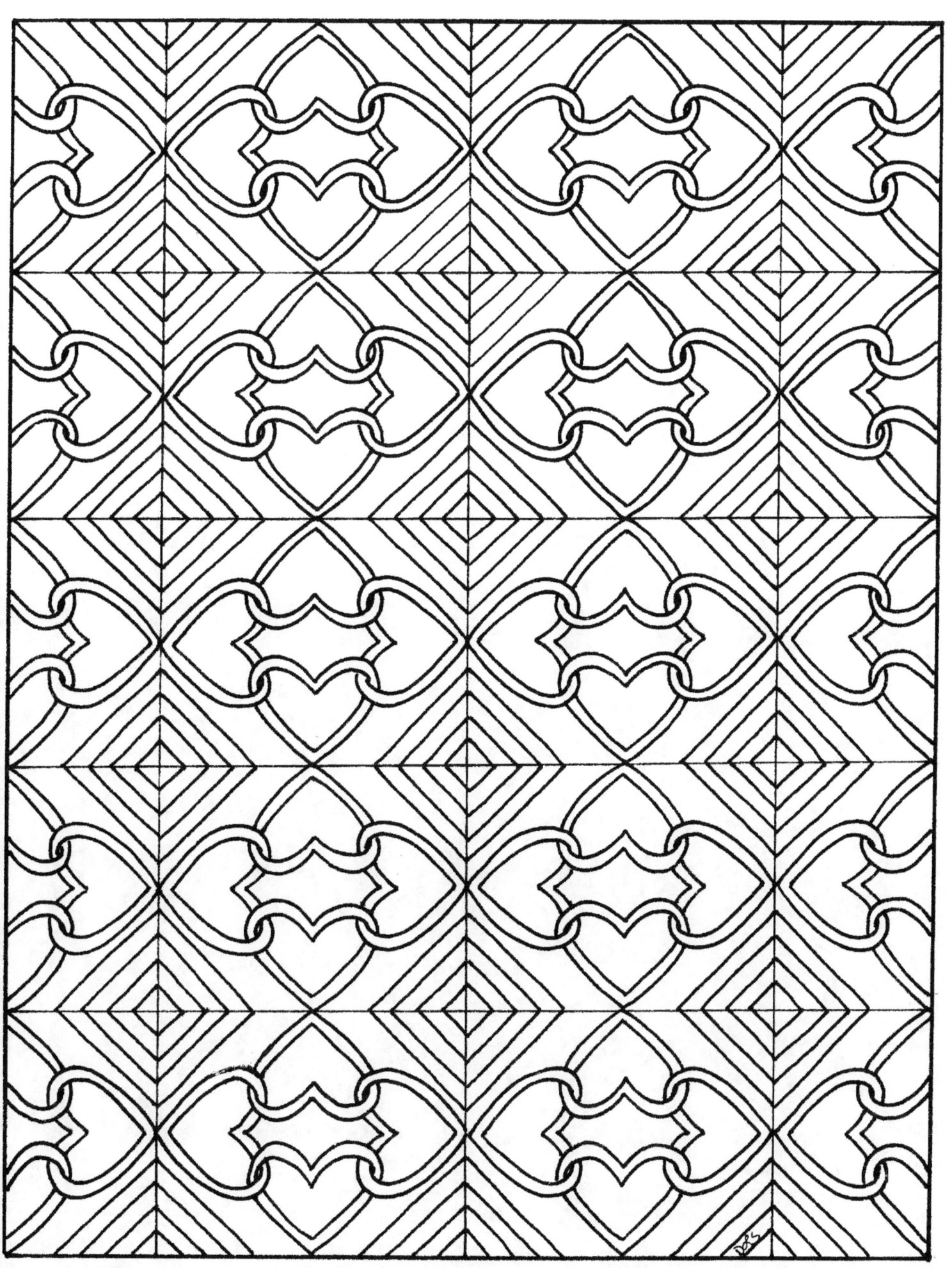

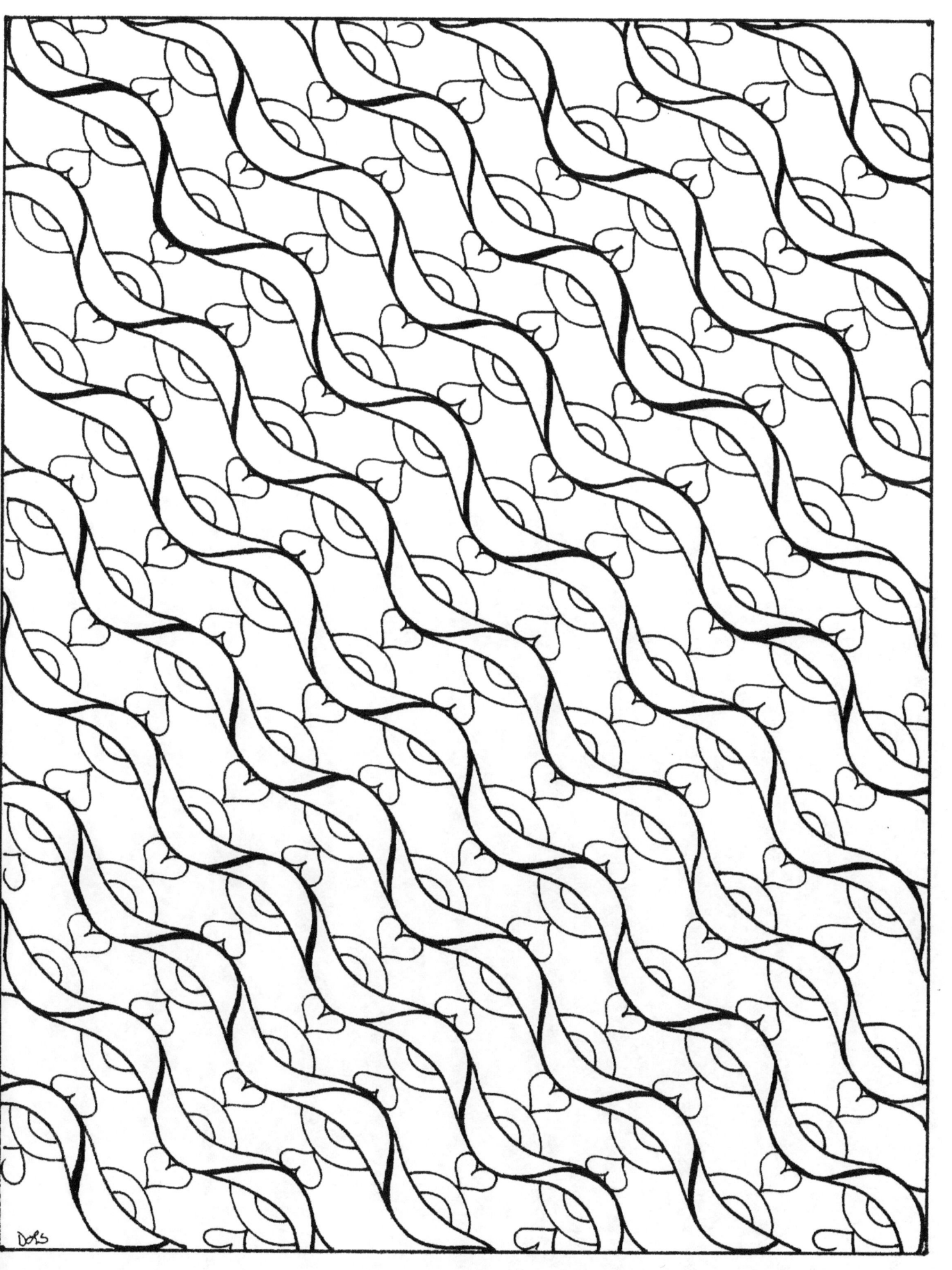

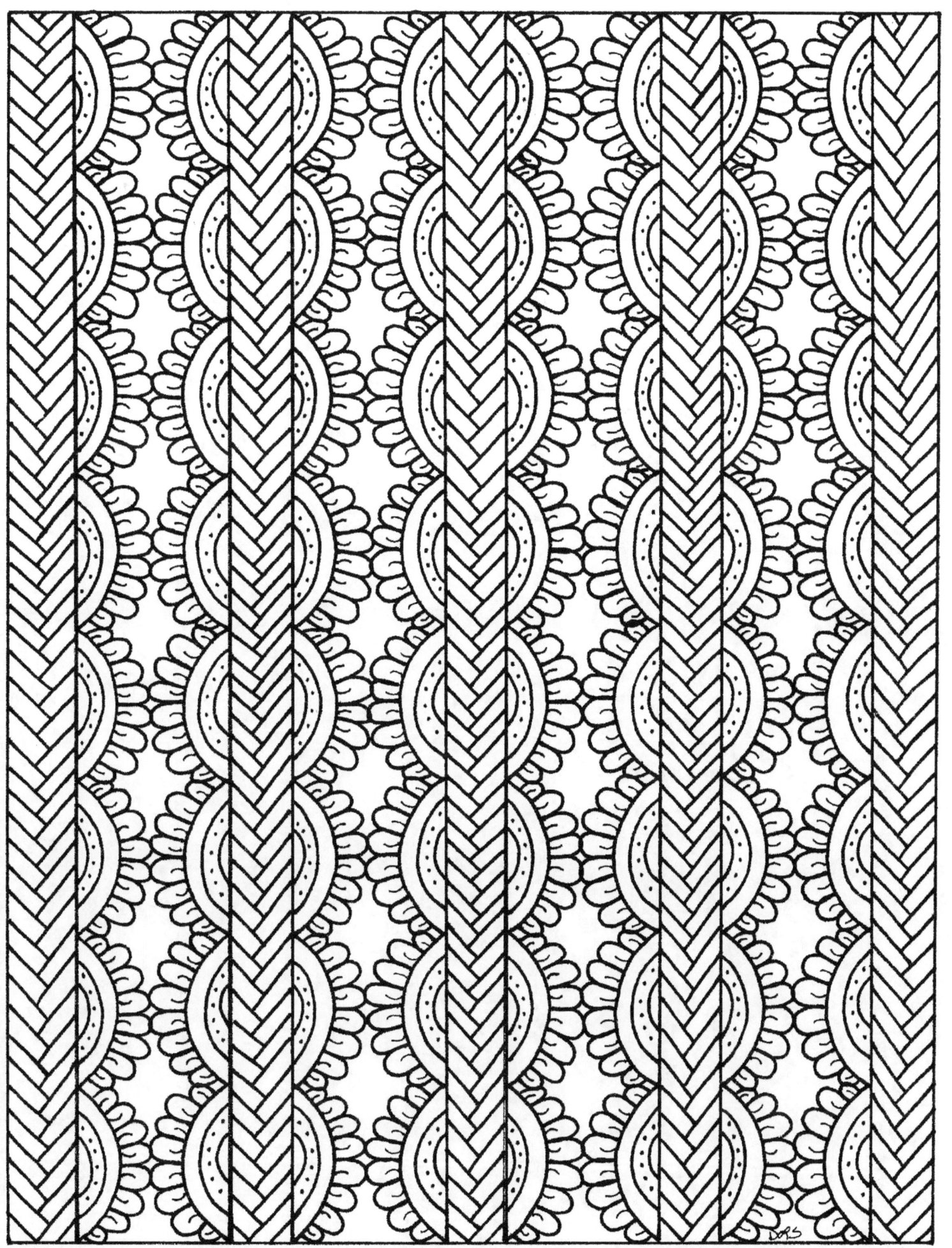

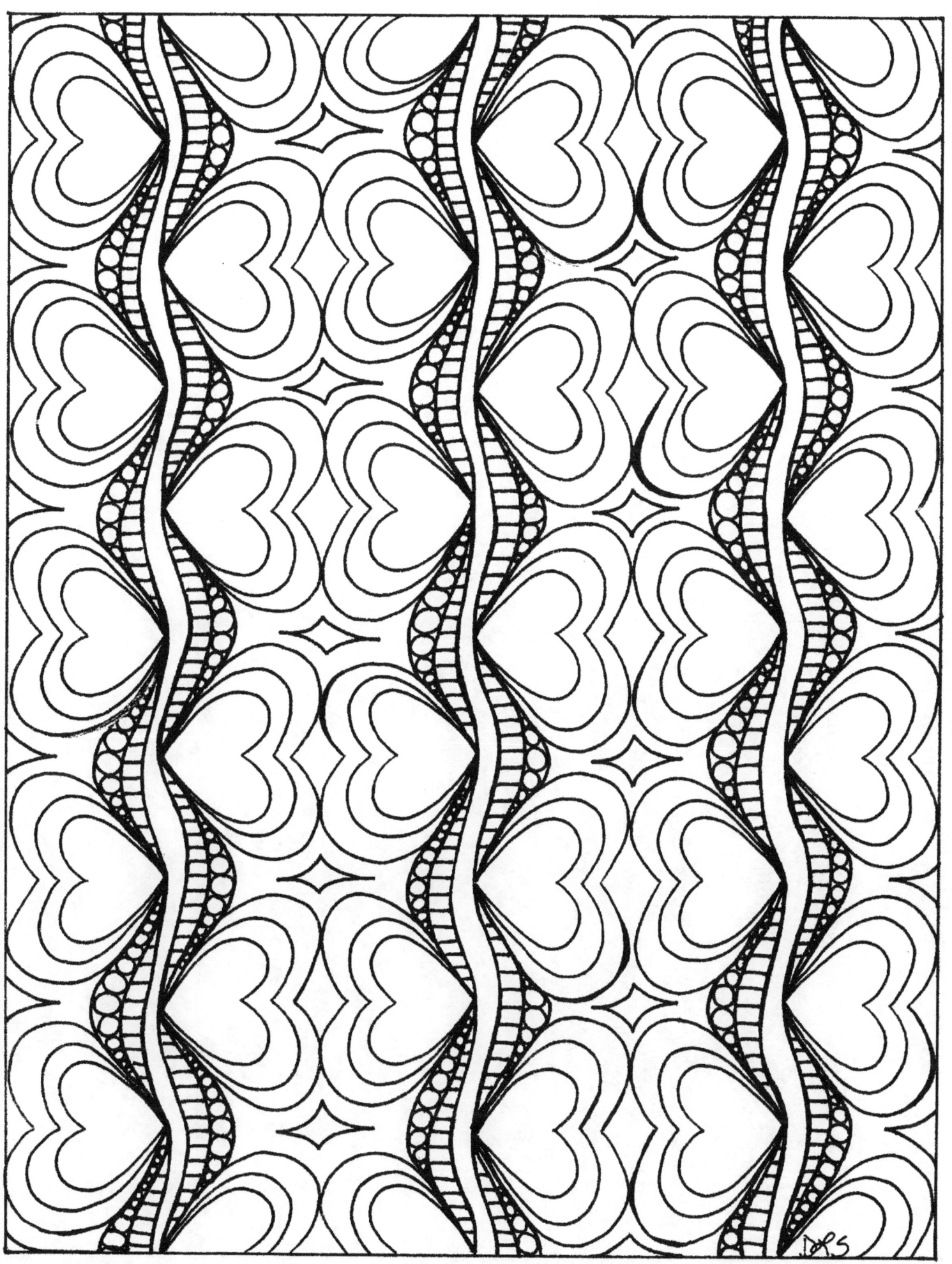

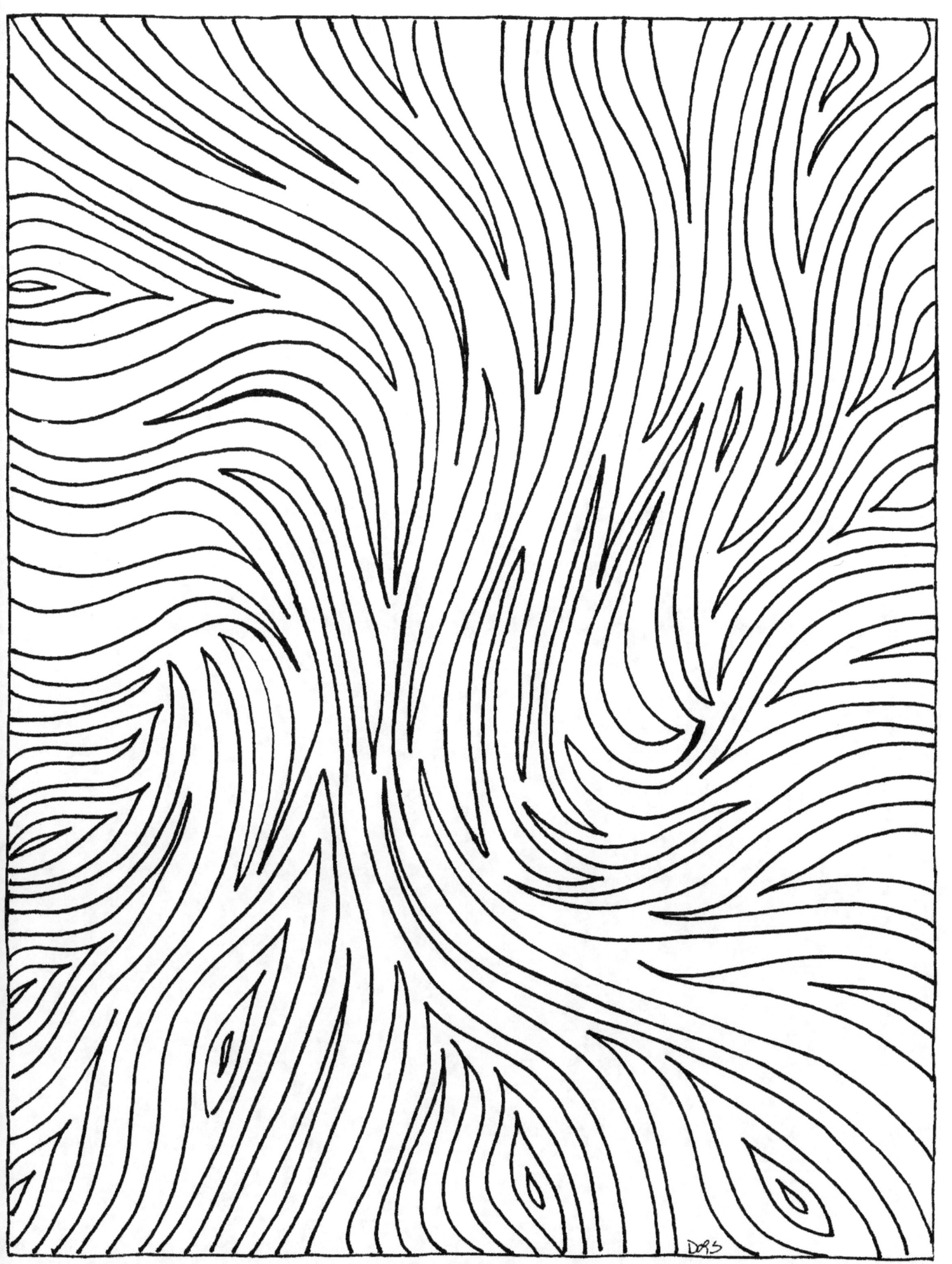

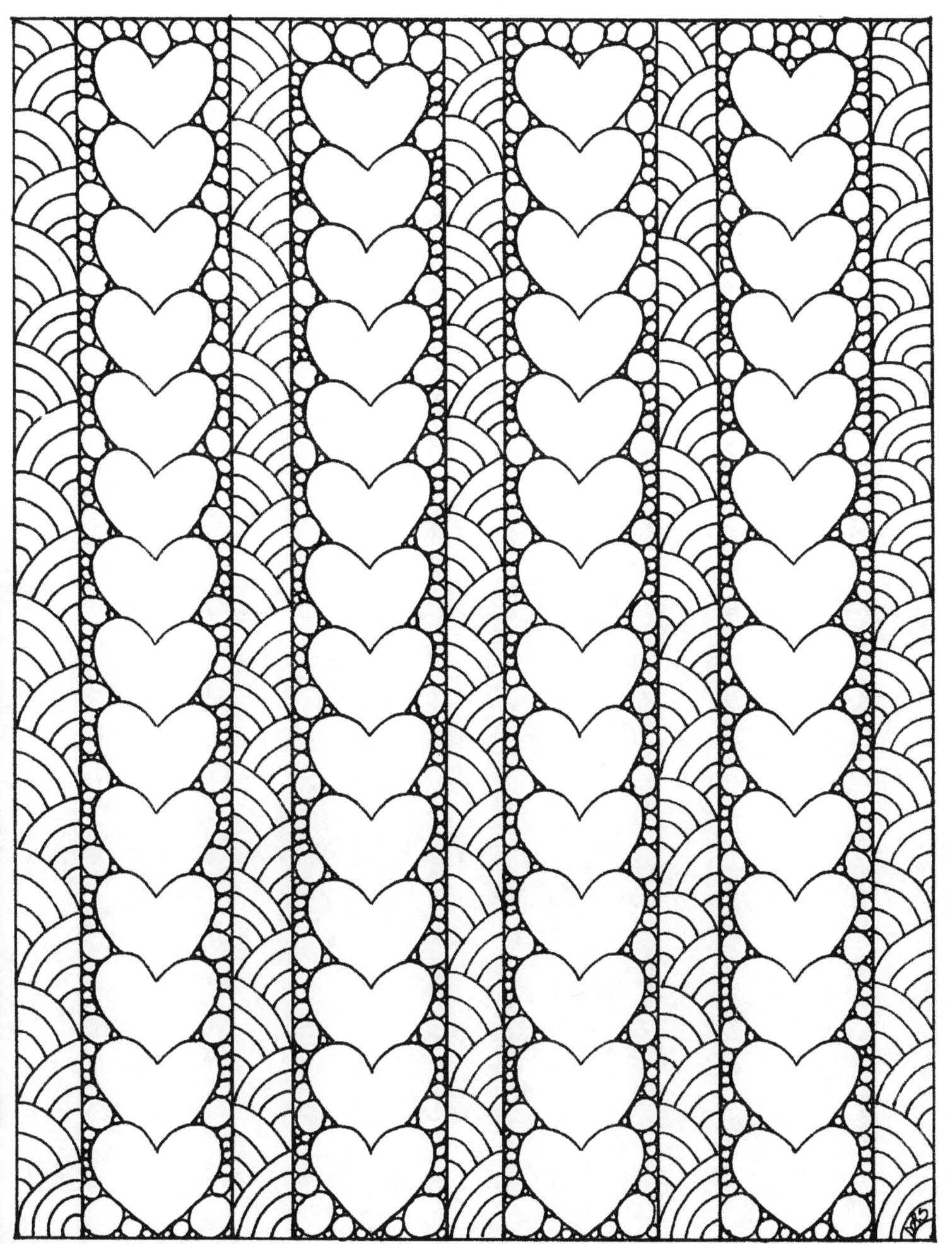

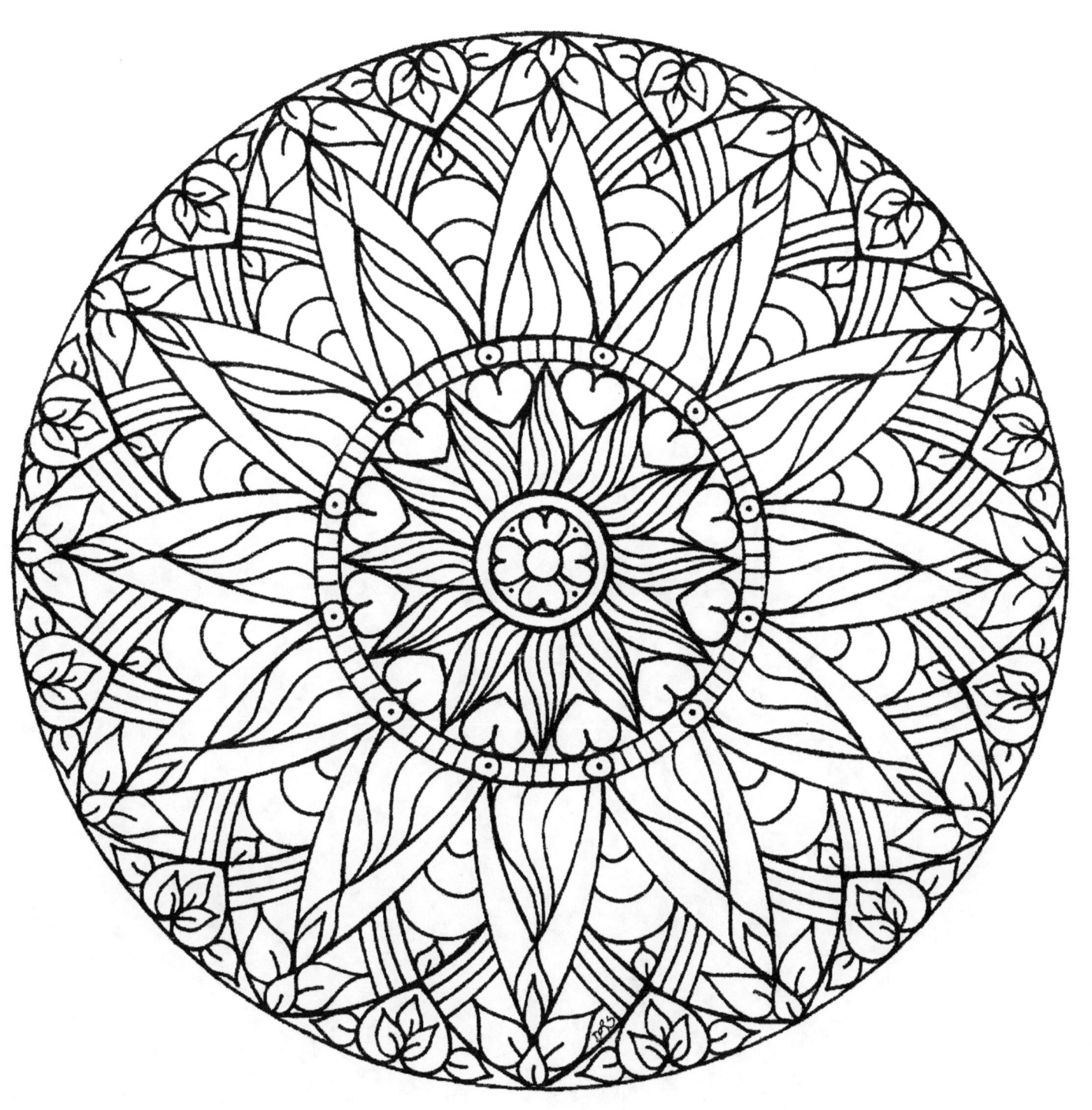

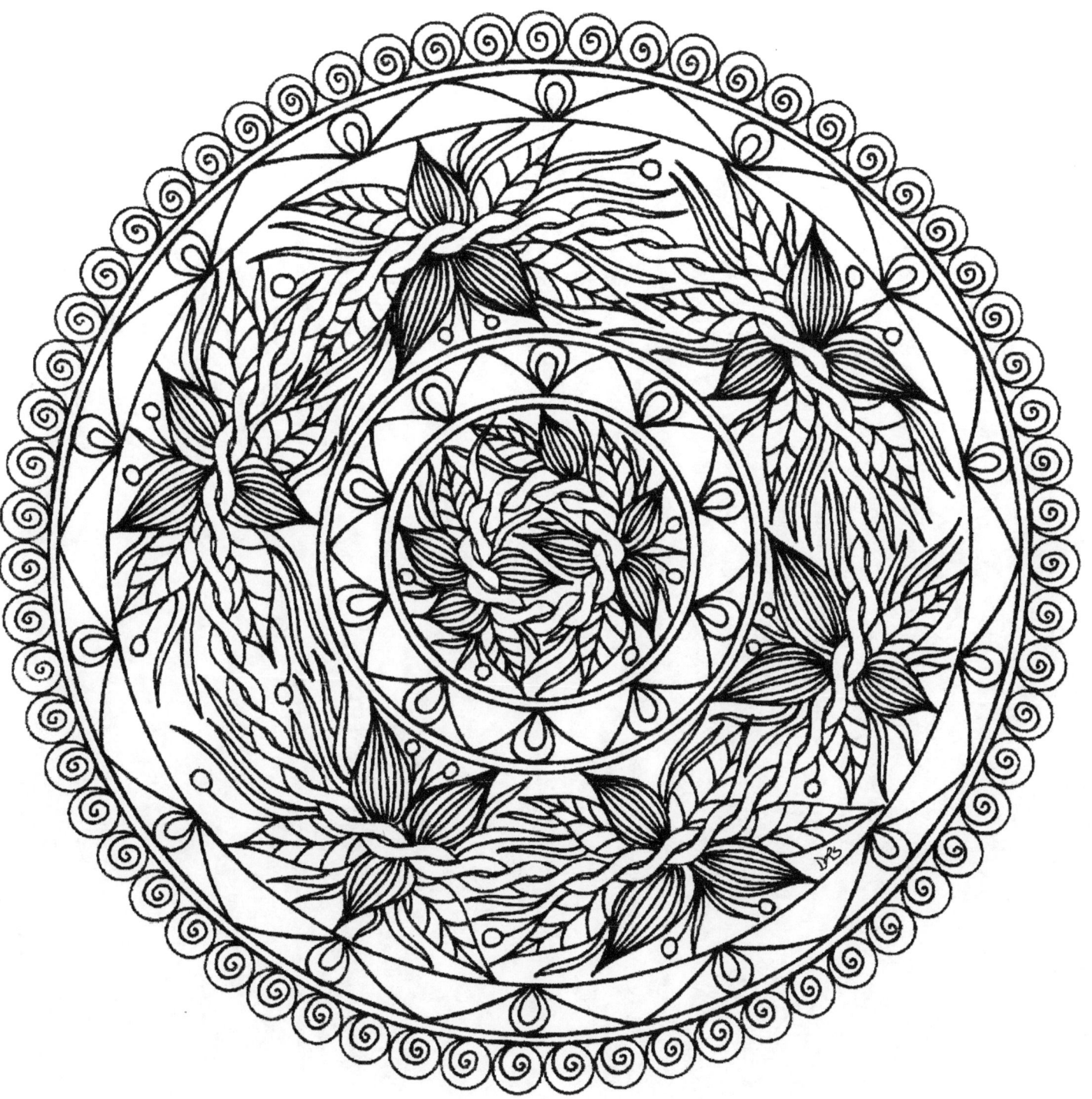

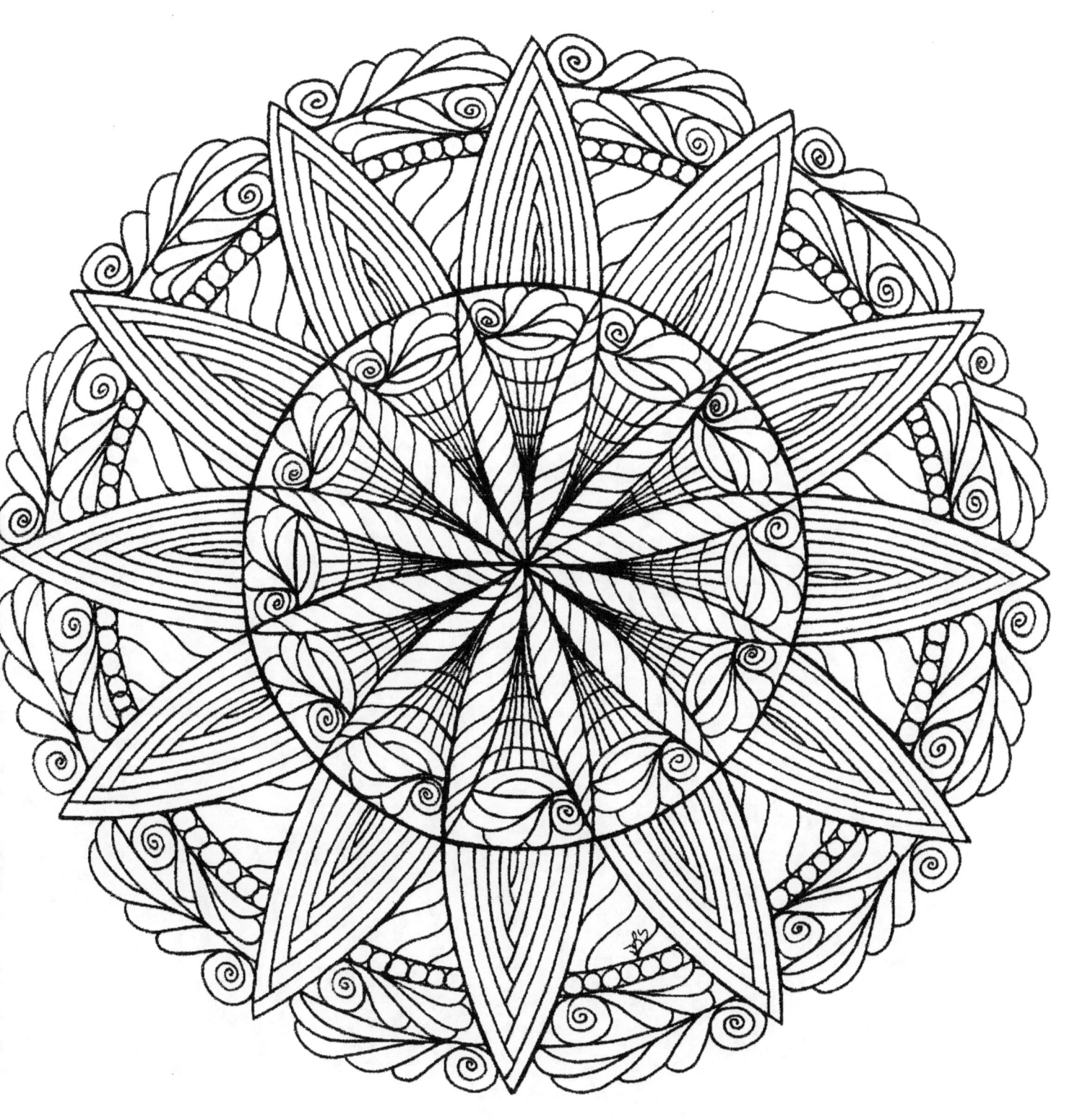

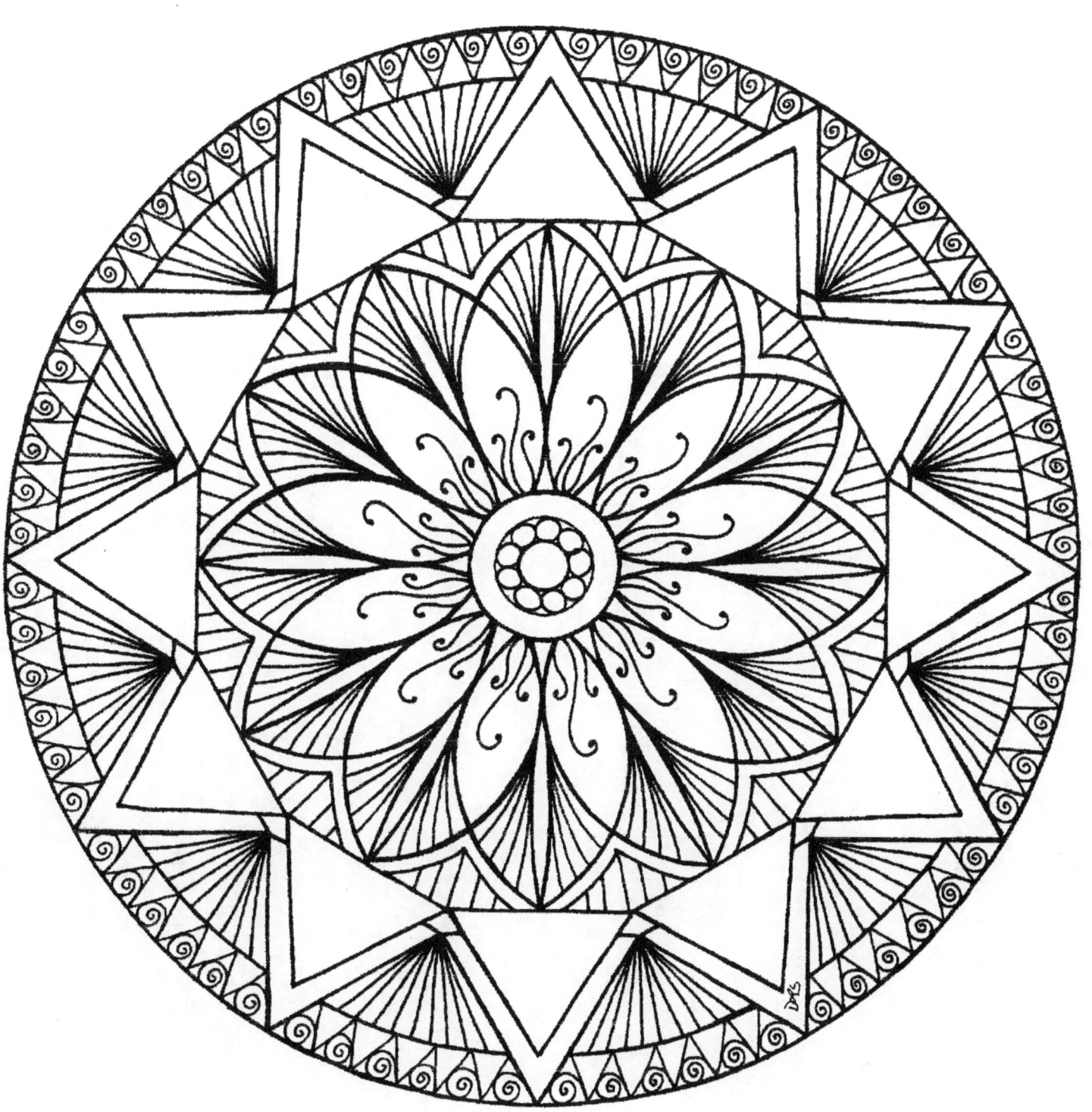

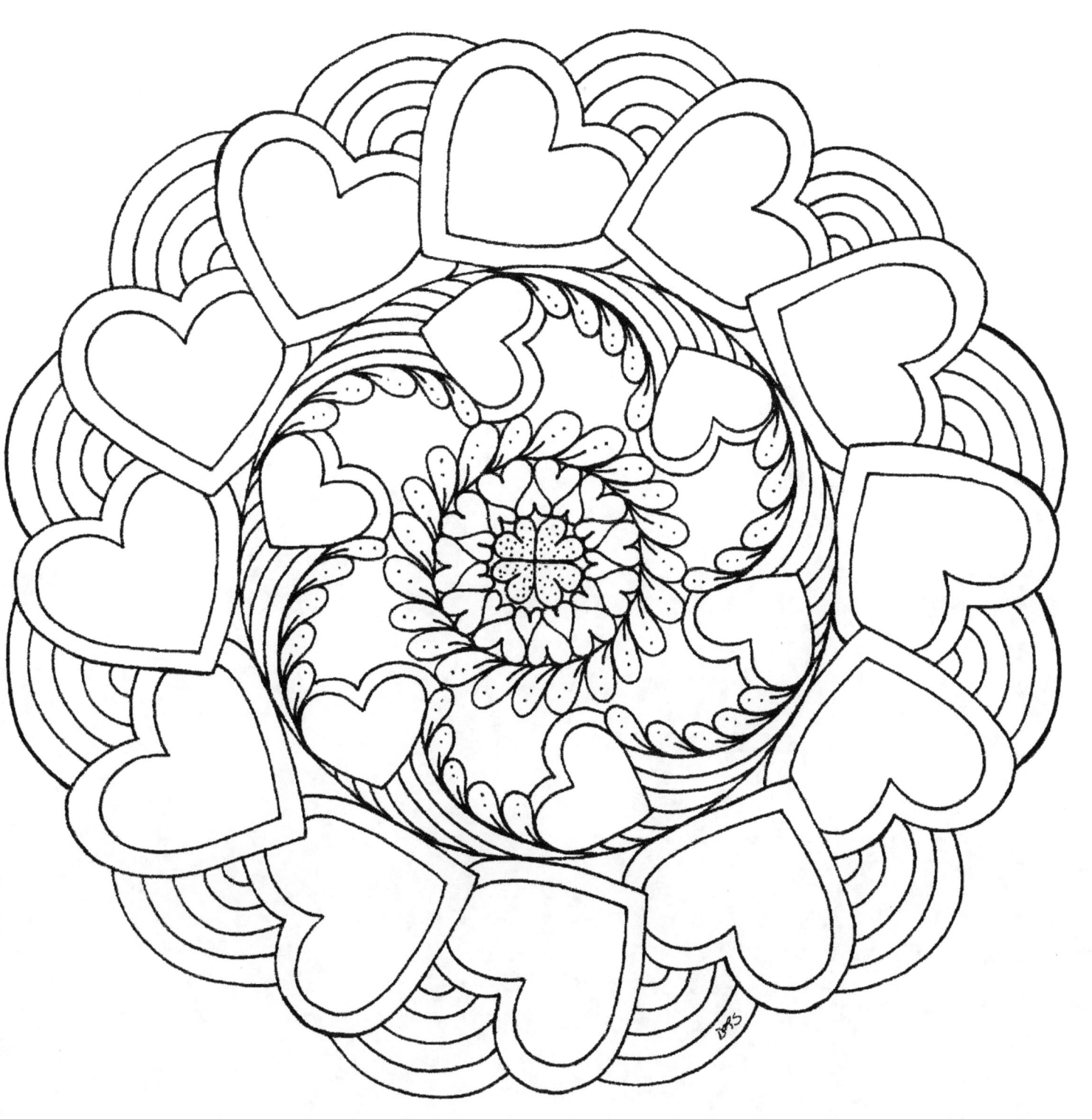

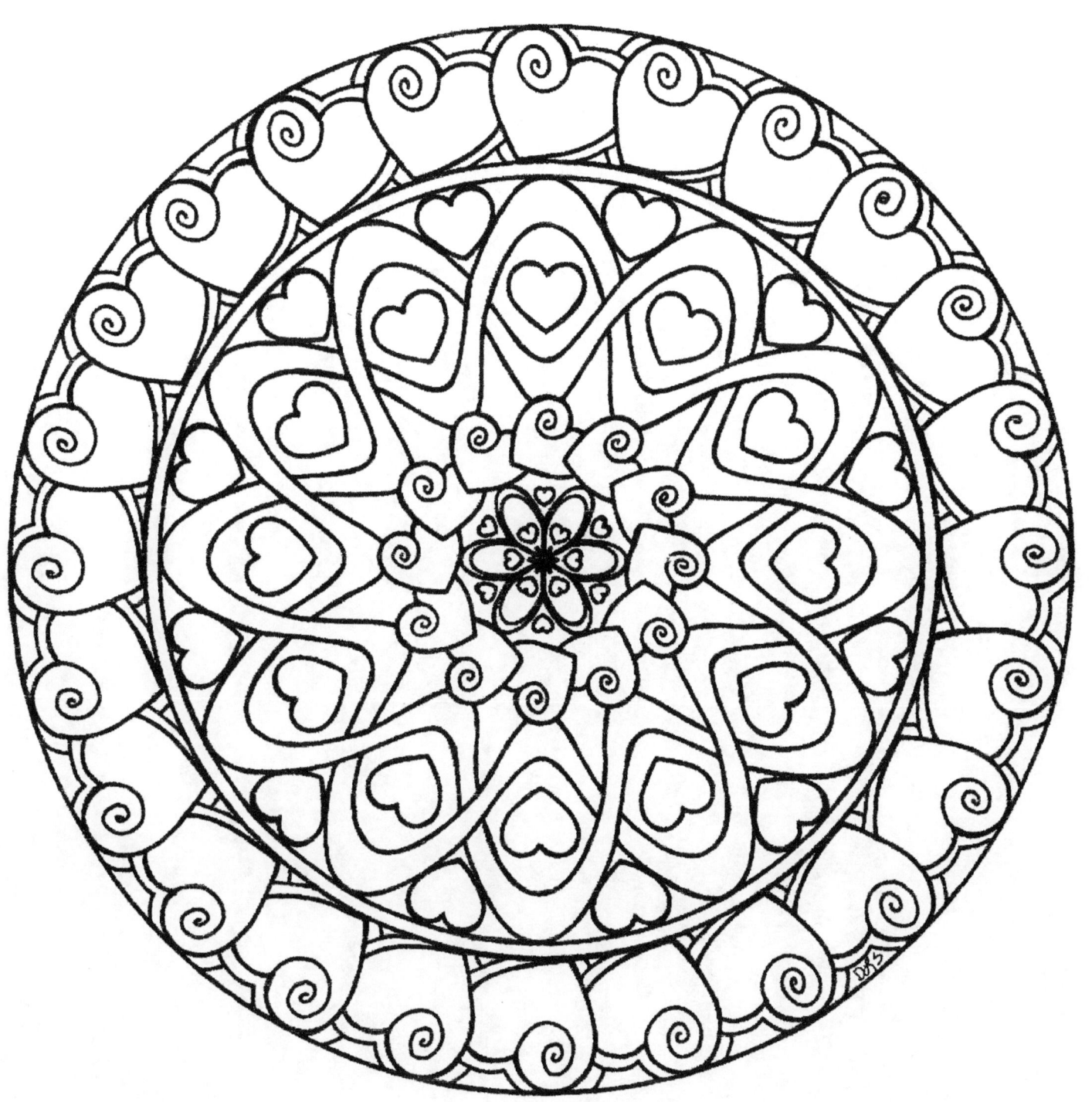

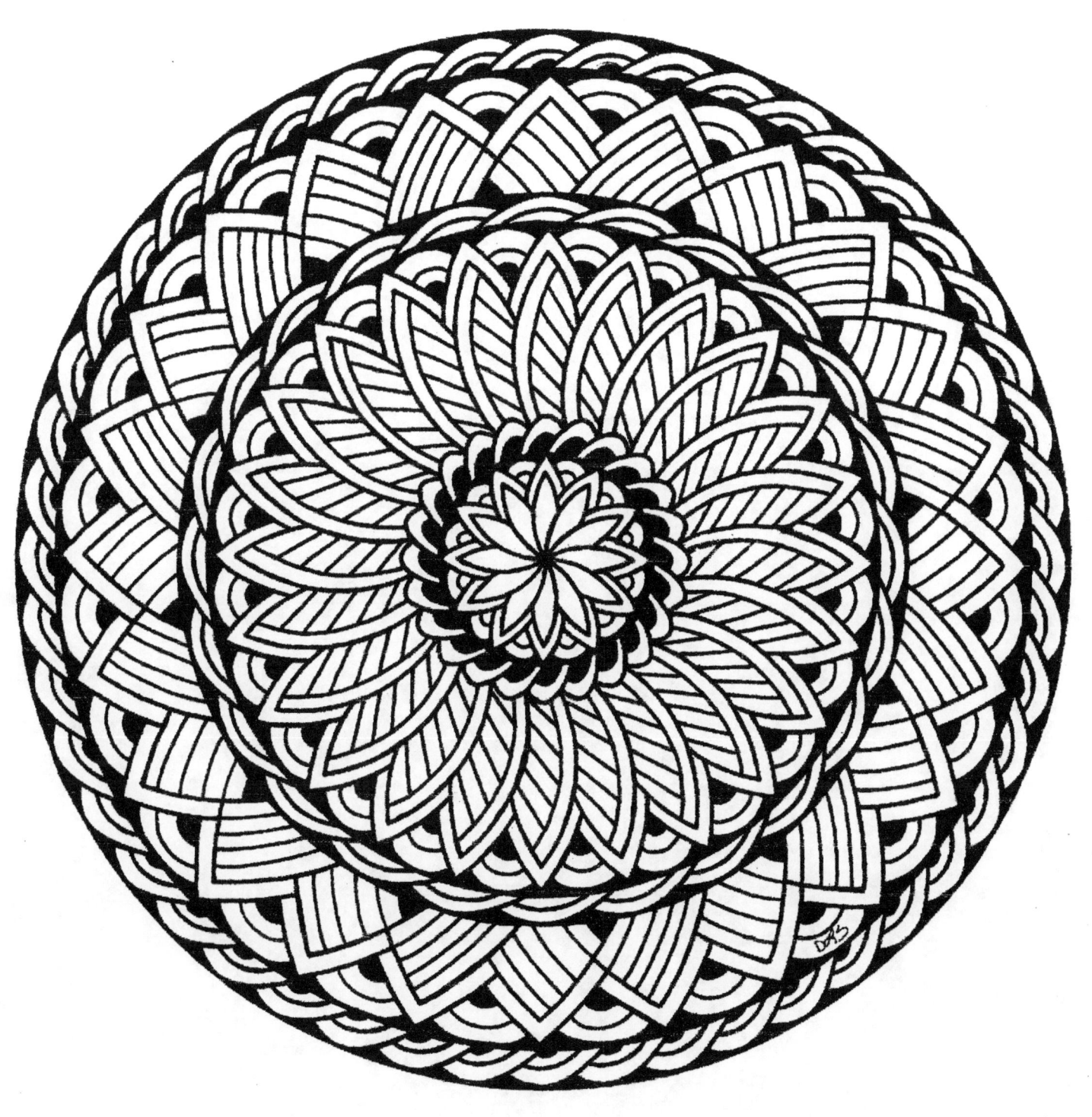

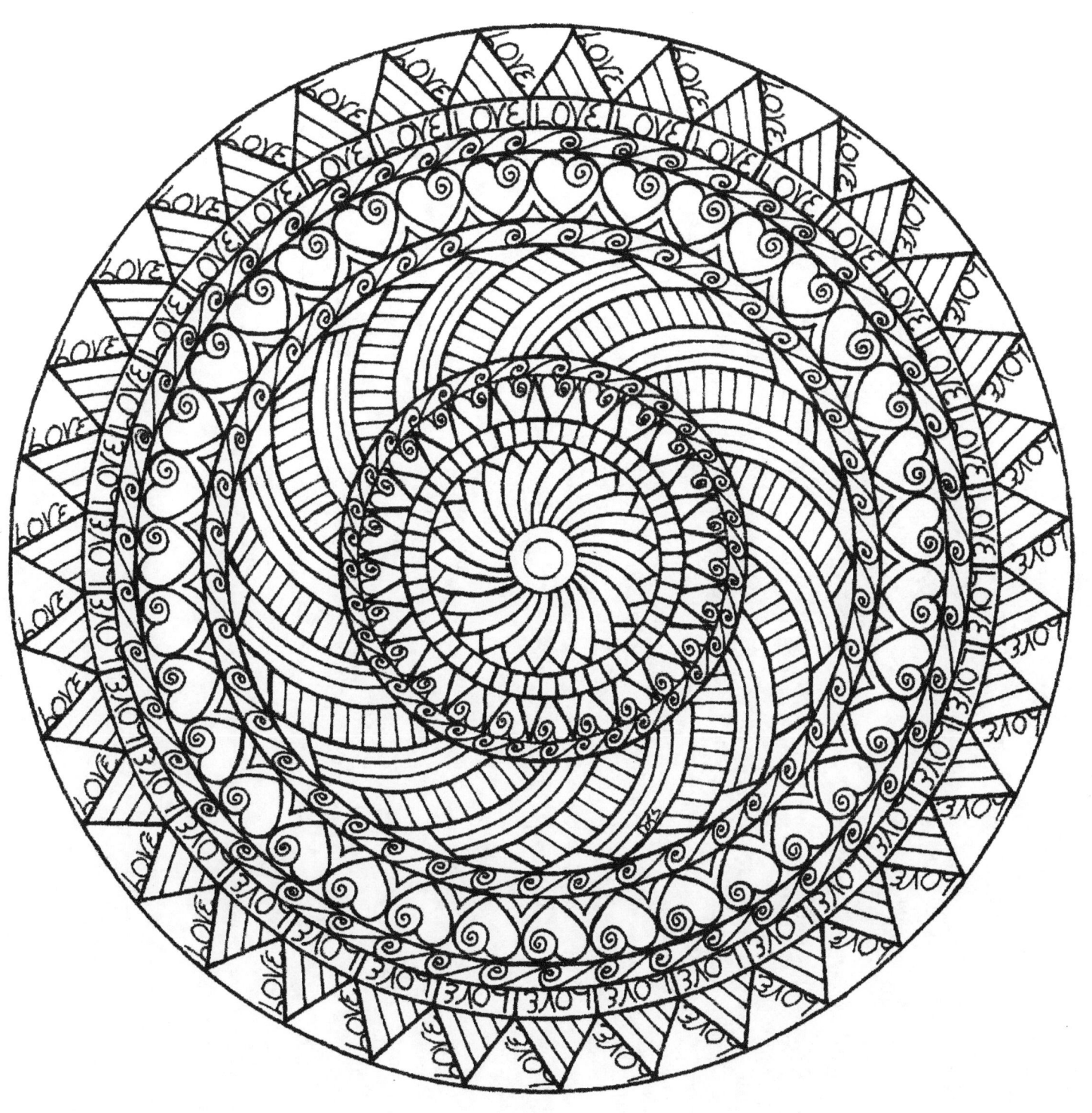

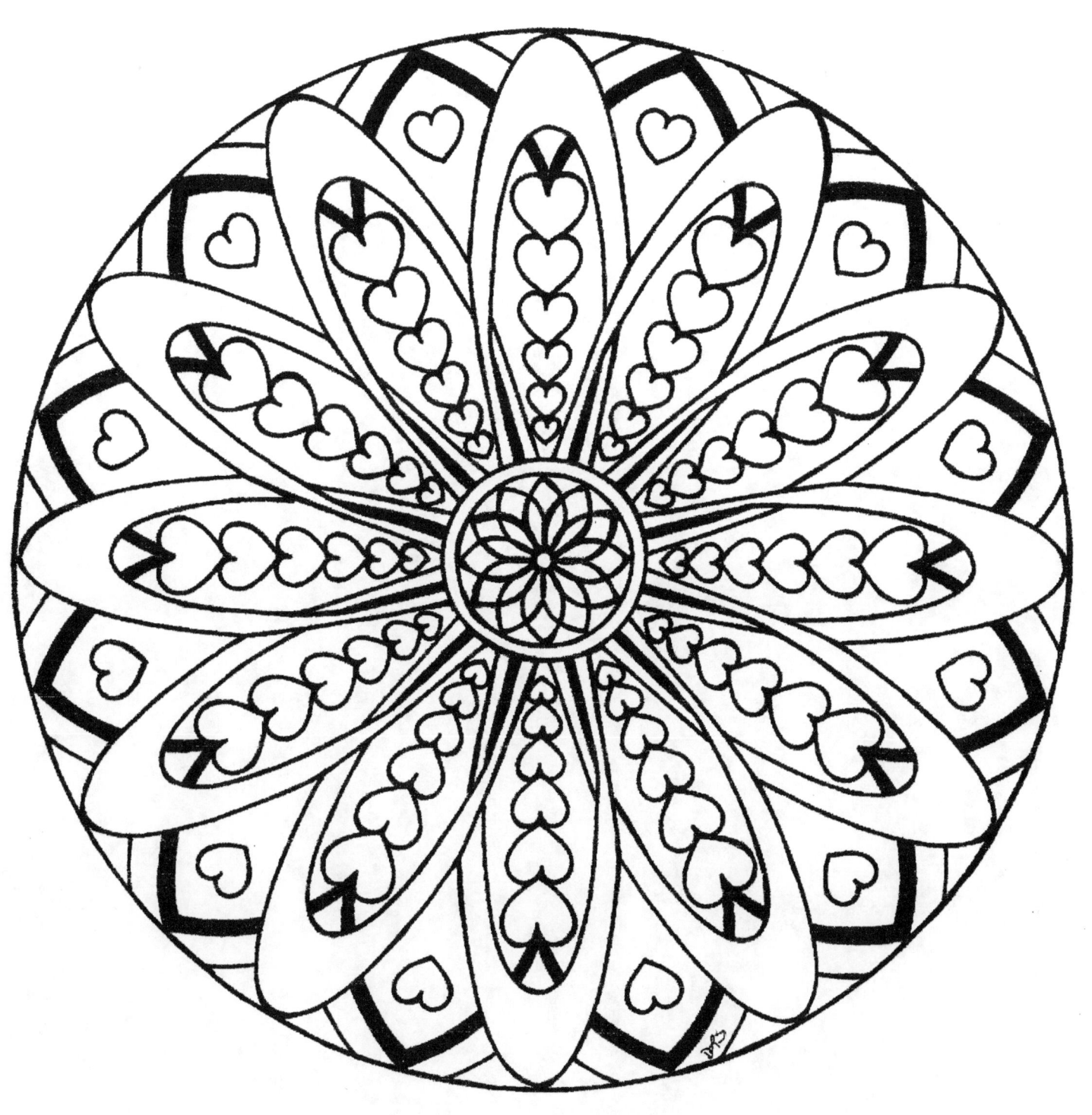

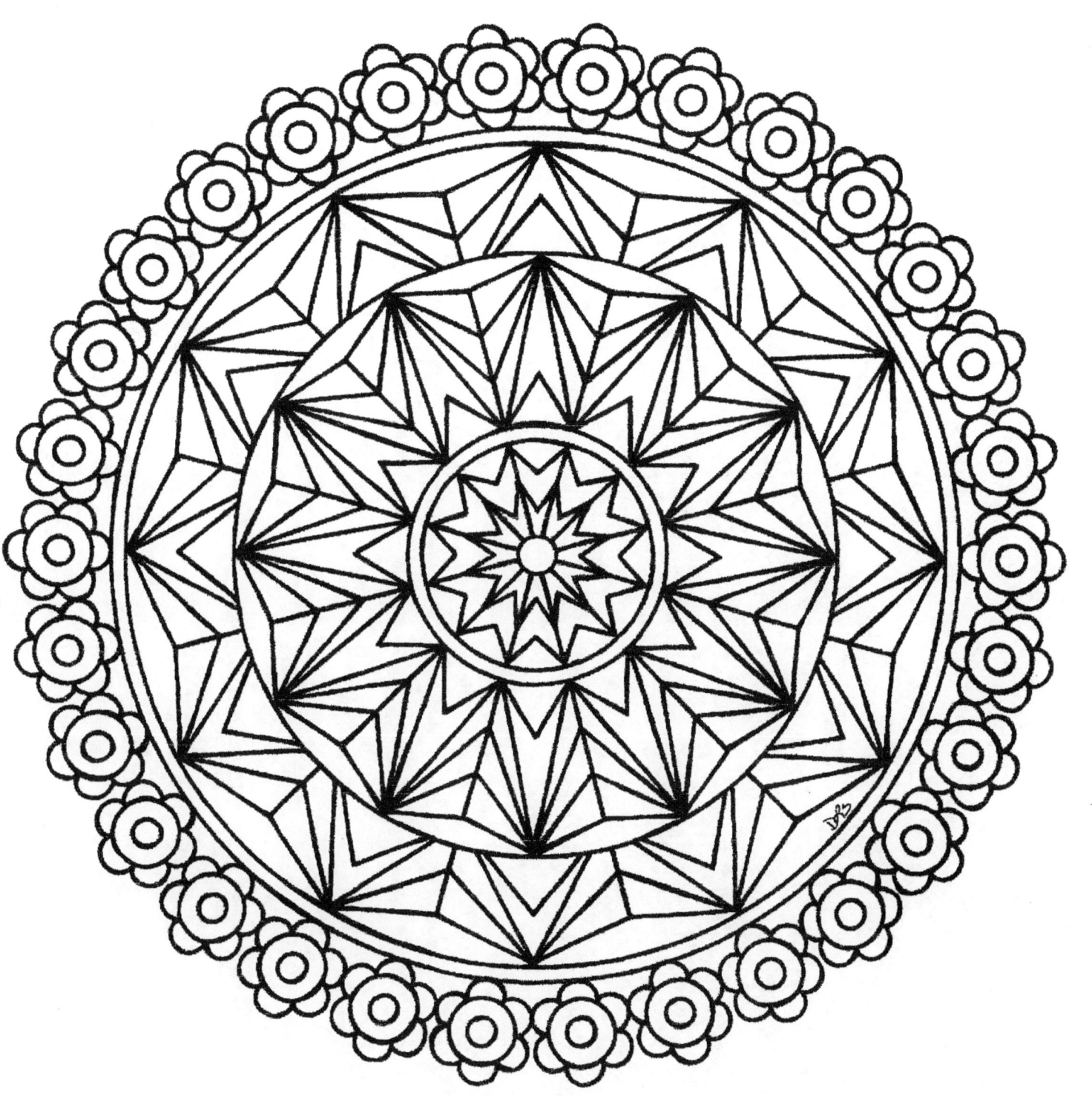

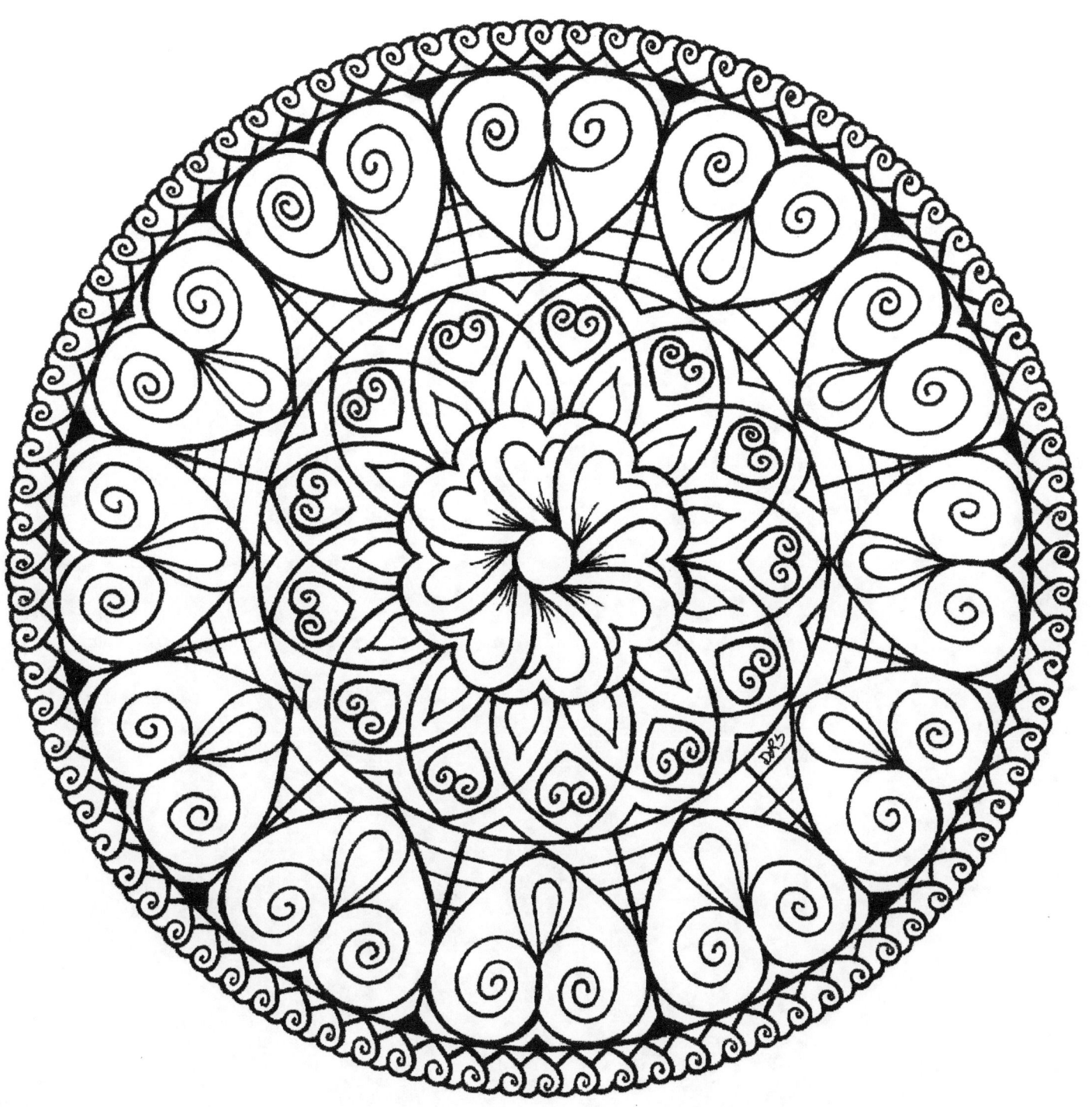

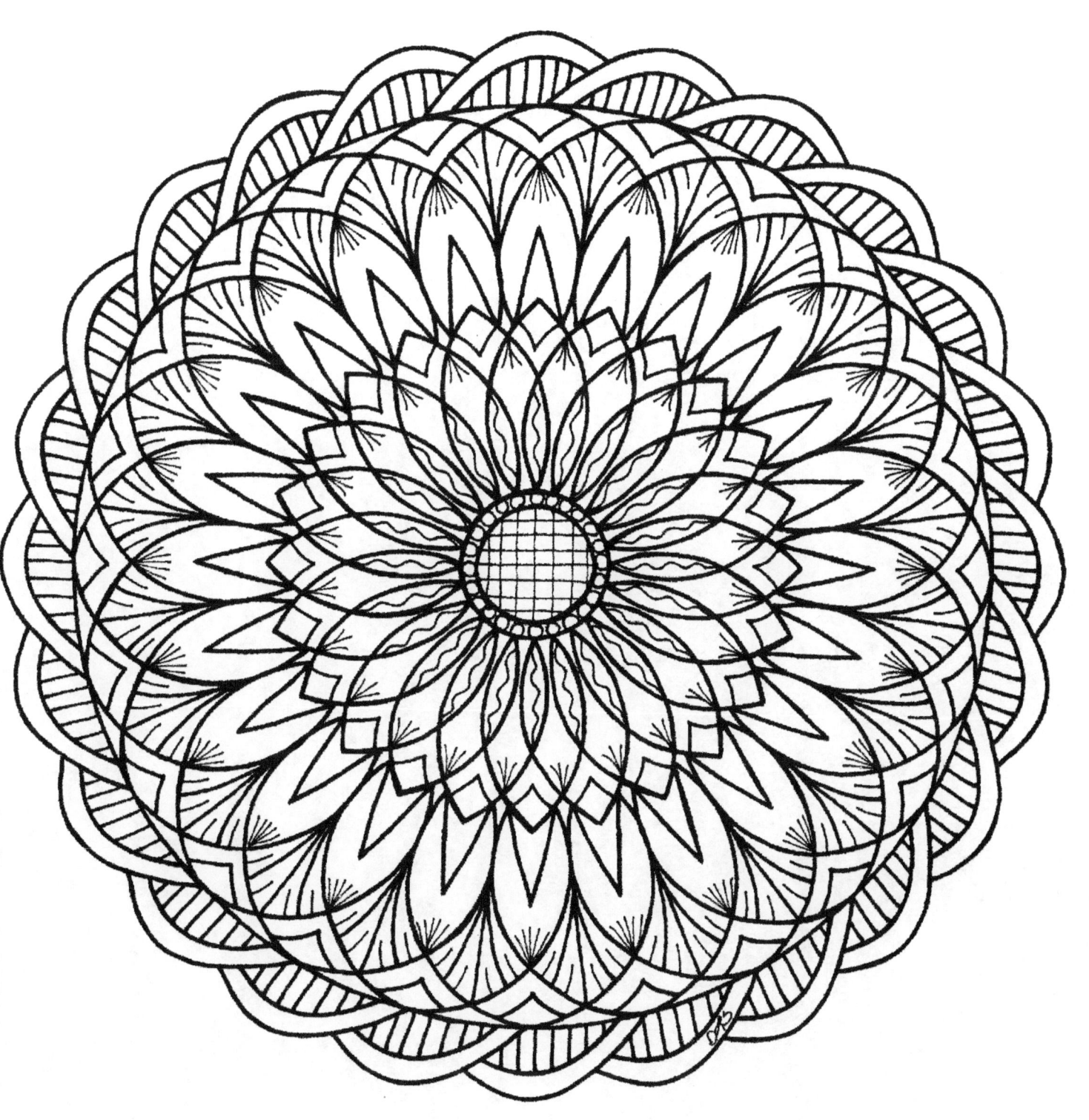

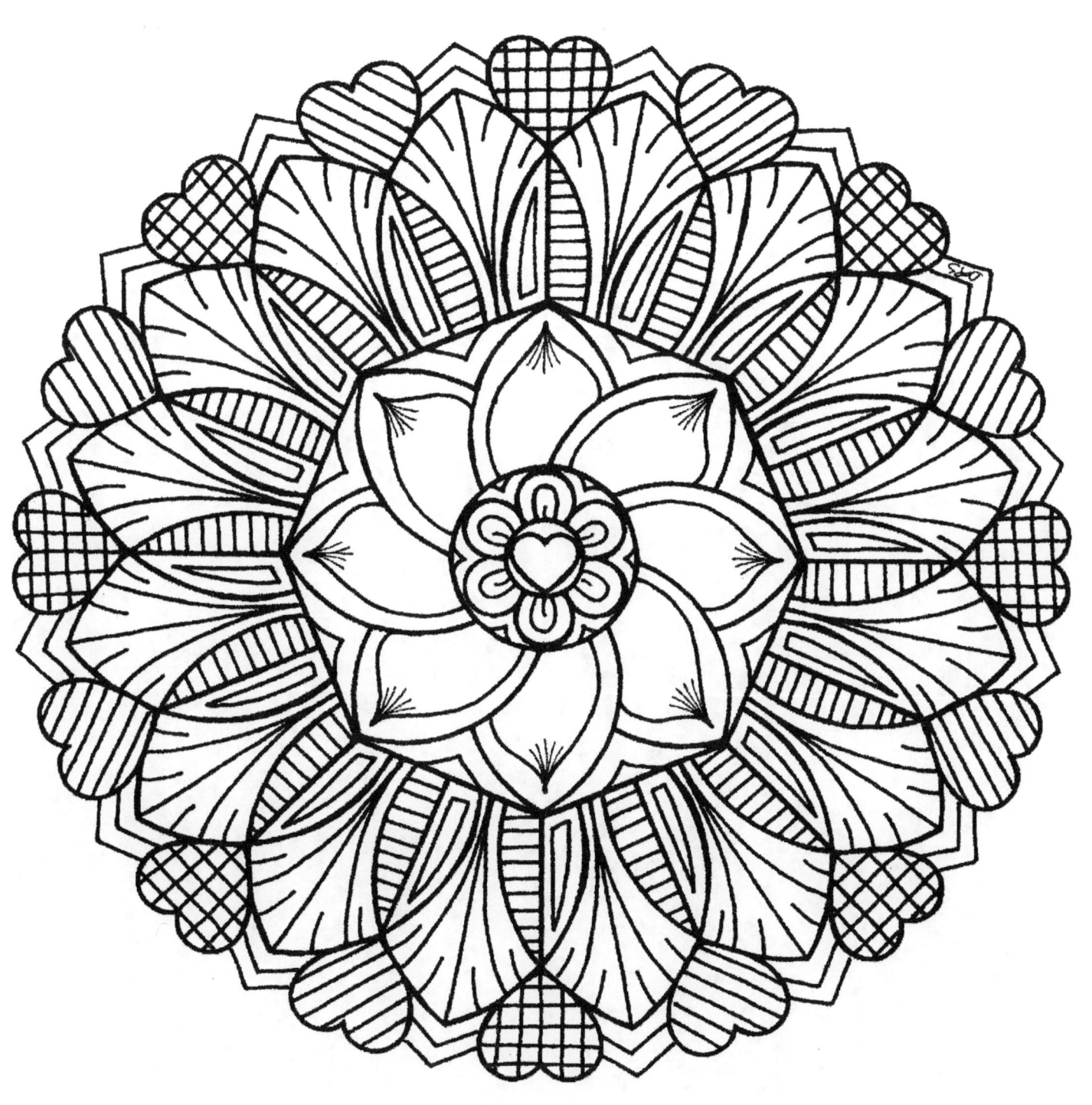